Football Passi
in
Black and White

By
Angie Stanger-Leathes

Published by Limelight Classic Productions Ltd
In association with Celebrity Football Passion Ltd

www.celebrityfootballpassion.co.uk

First Published in Great Britain in 2015 by
Limelight Classic Productions Ltd, Fort House, Old Hartley, NE26 4RL

A catalogue record for this book is available from the British Library

ISBN – 978-0-9560392-4-8

Printed and bound in North Shields by yourPrintDepartment.co.uk

Limelight Classic Productions Ltd
Fort House
Old Hartley
NE26 4RL

www.limelightclassics.com
Twitter : @footiepassion

Foreword

The Geordies stand as a beacon to loyalty, passion and, aye, a willingness to accept crippling disappointment.

Newcastle United are one of the best supported clubs in the land, despite being without a trophy of genuine note for more than 40 years.

They pack St James' Park with 50,000 plus every home game, a proud record for both club and city.

The author, herself a dedicated follower of the beautiful game, has spent much time with the famous and not so famous fans who help make football such a beloved sport.

This is the story of those fans – individual accounts in words and pictures of the undying passion they feel for those heroes who represent them. It has been lovingly put together over considerable time by Angie, with whom I have shared hopes and dreams through some torturous years following the Magpies.

This book is dedicated to other folk just like us.

John Gibson (Newcastle Chronicle)

To dream, the implausible dream

This fine tome is about the footballing passions of everyday folk. Now, some of those folks have an 'every day' that involves being in the public spotlight for assorted reasons, other folk have an 'every day' that involves the day-to-day slog of trying to ensure that the roof they wake up under the following morning, is made of tiles and not empty crisp boxes. Whatever their standing though, the mutual bond they share is the love of their football team. I class myself in the second category, although, I did share a flight home with Alan Shearer from Majorca one year, and by today's standards of celebrity, where caterwauling on television like a cat trying to give birth to a cactus plant, passes as singing super-stardom, I qualify in that category as well. In essence though, I am the soup before the main course, the Phil Jupitus before the Billy Connolly.

Thankfully ditching the cooking metaphor, I offer the date February 17th 1968. Whilst some readers were out whooping it up, celebrating the 10th anniversary of Pope Pius XII, declaring Saint Claire of Assisi the patron saint of television, I was setting foot in SJP for the first time. It was a testimonial for Jimmy Scott, and we beat Celtic 1-0. As a twelve-year-old, this was the biggest crowd I'd been in since the Woolworth's Boxing Day sale. The following year we won the Fairs Cup. Imagine, I'd been an attending supporter for less than two seasons, and we'd won a trophy. I thought it would always be like this! In my defence I also believed that eating my greens would be the making of me.

To some, the remembering of a particular date is triggered by a song, a holiday or the beginning/end of a romance. To me, the aroma of hundreds of pints of Exhibition, and the smoke of 20,000 Woodbines rolling across the stadium like a cartoon cattle stampede, evoke memories of that night. I won't bore you with statistics of matches watched over the years, away journeys to desolate Western and Southern hell holes, and finances expended in following my dream. Suffice to say, for the same outlay and mileage, Apollo 11 landed on the moon. I have celebrated a victory at Cambridge United like a lottery winner, stood saturated in the Gallowgate with 7,000 other rapidly shrinking die-hards on a biblically wet Wednesday watching half-a-game against Wrexham, and experienced the depths of despair at a defeat in the ludicrous play-offs to our deadliest rivals. Football is a drama greater than anything from Shakespeare, or even Holby City, because it is totally unscripted. There are inevitabilities, as we can readily attest over the last few decades. For example, when we somehow fall into a Wembley final, we never get to play Millwall or Bolton Wanderers, simply because we are usually the Millwall or Bolton Wanderers against Man United.

We also know that at the advent of every FA cup campaign, the opening credits of 'Match of the Day' will feature the wretched Radford fluking that shot, despite the fact that we were hardly the first victims of giant-killing. The programme also doesn't add the rider that, in the following game, we won at Old Trafford.

Whilst acquiring inordinate levels of cynicism over the years, I still have a deep affection for the game. I will sit and watch any game; indeed, last night I even watched women playing it! I often wonder whether, if I had been growing up in today's instant-fix society, I'd have had the tolerance or sheer nerve shredding-patience to stick with the club. I didn't really have any alternative 'pleasures' in my formative years as kids have today. They can access immediately a cornucopia of gaming technology and surf the internet to find diversions almost beyond human scope.

The total extent of my access to the wonderful world of technology was a Casio digital watch. I stared in wonder at it like Indiana Jones at the Ark of the Covenant. How do you explain to a ten-year-old today, at their first game, that we have embarked on another five-year plan, and that we are going to build slowly but resolutely? This is a demographic that taps its feet in frustration if their burger hasn't been delivered within three seconds, and that the world is collapsing around them if the internet page hasn't reloaded by the time they've exhaled. Because they grow up with instant gratification, kids cannot appreciate the transient nature of pleasures and pastimes, or indeed savour the unmitigated delight of an unexpected win at Chelsea. Or the gradual, growing excitement of a Cup run. This is a great sadness to me. I have lost count of the times I've tumbled in from a torturous, usually unsuccessful away trip, or trooped dejectedly out of a crushing home defeat and vowed dramatically to 'never darken your turnstiles again SJP' but a week later, like a junkie, I'm back for more. There is a huge part of me that wouldn't have it any other way.

There is a generation of Man United fans now, for example, who have never known the feeling of uncertainty at a game. They never need to consult the league table as they gorge on the silverware on offer. Theirs is usually a world of constant pleasure, but is it satisfying? The obvious answer as a Newcastle supporter is 'bloody right it is' but I'm not so sure. The Keegan playing years, followed by his first incarnation as manager, were the happiest of my days there. That is because it was an unusual departure for us - it could have gone either way, and the pessimists expected the worst. It worked though. He got us promoted on the back of his reputation as a player and manager. Whilst we missed the title by a Slimfast sandwich, the sheer joy of attending a football match in those days is something that I will treasure forever. They summed up football for me - it may at times provoke negative reactions; it may do the opposite; but at least it provokes a sentiment, a feeling, an emotion.

Once you learn that your blind date isn't always going to be Uma Thurman/ Johnny Depp with a bottle of champagne, and that sometimes it will be Goofy Glenda/Boring Brian from the Co-op with a karaoke invite, then you'll start to get it. All that's needed is to temper the joy with a soupcon of cynicism, and, like four hours of karaoke, the ecstasy will follow the agony.

This quote from Terry Pratchett probably encapsulates football passion nicely:

'The thing about football – the important thing about football – is that it is not just about football'.

And you don't get that killing cyborgs on a gamestation.

Paul Dixon, Gallowgate End

Chapter 1

The Birth of A Great Football Club

There are, on average, 50,000 devoted souls who attend every home game at St James' Park, home of Newcastle United. A remarkable feat considering the lack of a trophy in the living memory of most fans, but it wasn't always so, in terms of both great fan numbers and a shortage of silverware. In fact, Newcastle United Football Club owe their name, the birth of their historic club and huge fan base to a shortage of supporters watching the team formerly known as Newcastle East End. On 9th December 1892, a meeting at the Bath Lane Hall was called to address the 'lukewarm support' and after options such as 'Newcastle City' and simply 'Newcastle' were rejected as potential names for the new club designed to bring together the people of the entire city, 'Newcastle United FC' was chosen.

In terms of support, the newly named club never looked back and achieved its aim of uniting the fans of former clubs, Newcastle East End and Newcastle West End. A 6-0 demolition of Arsenal ensured St James' Park was off to a flying start in front of 2,000 supporters of *Newcastle United*—a great omen for the new club.

Fast forward a decade and Newcastle United had grown—from a fledgling side that had struggled to survive financially into the finest football team in England—and were regularly playing in front of 35,000 fans. The great

'Newcastle Away Supporters' tradition had its origins as far back as the side of 'Edwardian Masters' who won a hat-trick of First Division titles in 1904-05, 1906-07 and 1908-09. They also won the FA Cup,at a Goodison Park replay in 1910, after three lost finals at the 'cursed' Crystal Palace ground.

Fans in 1905 greet their team

For each final, Newcastle folk in their thousands took over an unsuspecting London with supporters resplendently displayed in black-and-white, arriving by car, rail or even steam boat. Men wore entire suits of stripes in the days before replica shirts—a few of whom had even walked all the way to the capital to follow their team and swelled the crowd to the more than 100,000 people who provided a great atmosphere. These devoted fans finally earned their reward when an Albert Shepherd brace delivered the FA Cup trophy to Tyneside and the team paraded it in an open-top tram to an unbelievable reception from the fanatical fans.

Gladstone Adams, Inventor and first 'famous' fan

A little-known fact is that the first prototype for the car windscreen-wiper was invented by Newcastle fan Gladstone Adams on his snow-swept way home from the Crystal Palace stadium, after seeing Newcastle United play Wolverhampton Wanderers in the 1908 FA Cup Final. He was travelling in his 1904 Daracq-Caron motor car and was frustrated at both the weather conditions and seeing his beloved team lose again in the Final. Adams—eschewing the traditional kick of a car-tyre to get things motoring—revolutionised car technology forever with a typical piece of Geordie ingenuity involving wood, rubber and a piece of string. The experience led him to invent the first prototype windscreen wiper. Although his version was never manufactured, it did inspire the original idea and his model is today displayed in Newcastle's Discovery Museum. Who says that necessity isn't the mother of invention? Adams was a prominent local figure and inventor in the North East and was also responsible for taking some of the earliest photographs of Newcastle United players (and a groundbreaking Selfie!), thus producing very early examples of football cards. A talented artist, 'Captain' Gladstone Adams as he was known, became Newcastle United's official photographer from the 1920s to 1950s.

Gladstone Adams

The first steps Newcastle United fans take to begin supporting their club are many and varied, yet often the tale consists of a father proudly taking his son—or increasingly in the modern game, daughter—to his or her first game. It is these magical starts in the life of a football fan that live so long in the memory and help forge the destined bond between a supporter and his club. Certainly, the effects of attending their first Newcastle United game can be life-changing and are often the beginning of a life-long love affair, as supporting the team becomes as natural as breathing. What Newcastle United really means to each fan is a very personal matter. Yet, that indescribable feeling when the team score a goal, win a match or sign a superstar, truly unites the fans as one.

Portrait of a player by Gladstone Adams

Football has been compared to religion and—if a lifetime of daily devotion, prayers and blind faith, and the continued investment of hard-earned cash is anything to go by—Newcastle United certainly has a devout and faithful following. Interestingly, many of the historic football clubs in England were teams set up originally by the church with the aim of improving community spirit, especially amongst young men. The club has certainly helped forge a bond between people in Newcastle and beyond, providing strangers with instant common ground for conversation and friendship—no matter what else may separate them. This is a tradition that has carried on around the world and the sight of a Geordie wearing his famous black-and-white stripes has often opened the door to a warm welcome in many of the far-flung corners of the globe. Wherever you go in the world, you are never far from a Newcastle United fan.

At the start of the First World War in 1914, the government took over St James' Park and stables were erected in the stands. However, the 1914-15 season kicked off as normal and football was seen as a welcome distraction from a war that was expected to last just a few months—instead it dragged on for four years. The crowds were swelled with the inclusion of Lord Kitchener's Armed Forces. As the seriousness of conflict became apparent, shooting practice of the football kind was replaced by rifle ranges at St James' Park, with many of the United players drafted in and some providing a deadlier shot with a gun than with a ball! The ground was used for rallies and exhibition games to raise money and to recruit local fans into the army. 27 of the team's playing squad of 40 went away to serve in the Great War and, sadly, many did not return. However, this didn't deter the football faithful from showing typical football passion. A Christmas Day and Boxing Day feast of derby day games against Sunderland gave fans a real festive treat, with Sunderland winning 5-2 at St James' Park and Newcastle returning the favour with a 4-2 win at Roker Park. For the remainder of the war, Newcastle United and St James' Park was all but shut down as travel logistics and the ravages of war made it impossible to even compete in the local leagues, but it was back with an almighty bang when 40,000 folk saw Newcastle United take on South Shields in 1917. Normal service had resumed.

1920s and 1930s

The Geordies made history as the first away fans to visit new stadium Highbury, and a 55,000 crowd watched Newcastle United beat Arsenal by a goal to nil, which spoilt the party for the Londoners. A post-war soccer boom was in the making and the crowds and Newcastle were back in business. Again, the derby game proved the top draw on Tyneside, with a crowd of 61,761 setting a new club record attendance. The 1924 FA Cup Final between Newcastle and Aston Villa was a cacophony of noise and a riot of colour, due to the bells, bugles and wooden rattles employed like never before and large-scale black-and-white banners joined scarves for the first time along with stuffed magpies. A 2-0 win sent the fans back to Tyneside in a state of delirium.

In the late 1920s, Newcastle had their first true superstar—Hughie Gallagher—and the famous tradition of number 9 shirts being worn by famous centre forwards was born. A legend on the pitch due to his goal-scoring prowess, and a colourful figure off it in the pubs of Newcastle, the wee Scot acquired legendary status. He was captain of the team that won the 1927 First Division League title and was top goal-scorer with 39 goals. He was the toast of Tyneside and cast the famous number 9 striking mould that Jackie Milburn, Malcolm Macdonald and Alan Shearer would fill in later years. Stan Seymour, who would play for, manage and become a Director at the club once said 'The ordinary rules didn't apply to Hughie Gallagher because he was a soccer genius'.

Newcastle kicked off the 1930s with their all-time record crowd, 68,386, on 3 September 1930, for Hughie Gallagher's return with Chelsea, the club he signed for at the end of the previous season. Happily for the fans, Newcastle won and it was a magnificent day for the huge crowd. Significantly, the very first Newcastle United Supporters Club was formed in 1930 and following the team became a serious, organised business.

In 1932, the team won the FA Cup again thanks to a disputed offside goal against Arsenal, although the club were forced to cancel pioneering 'European' overseas exhibition games in Paris and Hamburg, as flying was deemed to be too dangerous at the time. In the late 1930s, the team suffered a decline and were relegated to Division Two.

1940s

During the Second World War, the football was a real treat for fans and a welcome distraction from the rationing and realities of conflict. There were goals aplenty on an unprecedented basis, with 11-0 wins against Middlesbrough and Bradford and a 6-6 Tyne 'derby' draw with Gateshead. Whilst lacking the rigorous high standards of football in peacetime, the games were relished by the fans and made for an extra sense of community for all concerned, players and fans alike. In fact, there was always the unique chance you could be picked out of the crowd if the team were short of players—and actually play for the Magpies! Future England stars like Tom Finney and Stan Mortensen 'guested' for Newcastle United, while local hero Albert Stubbins scored 232 goals in 188 games and a total of 122 goals were scored in the 1944/45 Regional League season. The team competed in the 'War Cup' instead of the FA Cup in front of 30,000. Whilst not managing to make it 'Wor Cup', they did manage to assert local supremacy by winning the Tyne-Wear-Tees Cup in 1944, when a certain young Jackie Milburn scored the winning goal 32 minutes after extra time finished. It was a case of 'next goal wins' and Newcastle won the bragging rights that particular time. Goals by the hundred, international stars on display, the chance to play for the team and local domination—Hitler even spared the stadium while bombing Roker Park—there were worse things than being a Newcastle United fan in World War II.

After the war ended, Charlie Crowe in 'A Crowe Among Magpies' recounts that a pre-season practice game between two teams from the Newcastle squad drew a crowd of 27,763. Charlie called this 'amazing' and no one can disagree with that description. Football's popularity was sky-high once peace returned to our country and crowds of up to 60,000 crammed into the stadium on match days. Frank Watt, Newcastle Club Secretary, had his own way of measuring the crowd, as he told Charlie Crowe from his vantage point 'Well Charlie, when I can see their chests clearly then about 30,000 are present; when I can see their chins then that means 50,000; but if I can see only the whites of their eyes then I know we have 60,000 plus inside St James' Park'. There were plenty of times when Watt could only see the whites of supporters' eyes. Newcastle set their record average attendance in 1946/47 with a crowd average of 52,699—a magnificent achievement.

Newcastle and Charlton fans with rattles, FA Cup game January 1948

Chapter 2

1950s Glory Days

If wartime football was a fun and light-hearted distraction from the grim realities of war, yet lacking the intensity of the real thing, then the post-war boom and Newcastle's domination of the 1950s was the tonic the Magpies had fought hard for. Local hero 'Wor' Jackie Milburn helped the Magpies to a hat-trick of FA Cup victories in 1951, 1952 and 1955. Huge crowds at St James' Park were commonplace and, more often than not, 60,000 fans would stream into the ground, as the magic of football's oldest competition captured the imagination of the Tyneside public. The fans followed the team in their thousands to away games and, ultimately, to Wembley Stadium no less than three times during the 1950s. Wembley stadium averaged 100,000 fans for every cup final played there, with the number of Newcastle fans attending estimated at between 15,000 and 30,000. Such numbers were put somewhat into perspective, however, when the players returned to Tyneside with their silverware, and more than 200,000 proud Geordies lined the streets in those glorious years to welcome their returning heroes. The entire city celebrated each magnificent cup win and it was smiles all the way for the Tynesiders, in what were difficult post-war times. The club cemented its place in the hearts of the Geordie faithful, and the quality of life for the fans was enriched by the magnificent exploits of their beloved team. Cup-winning team captain, Joe Harvey, was amazed by the sheer passion of the Tyneside public when the team returned triumphant in

1951, having just won the FA Cup by virtue of a 2-0 win against Blackpool. He said 'We knew we would get a terrific reception, but I never imagined it would be like this. It was wonderful'.

Fans welcome 1951 FA Cup Winners

1952 saw 10,000 fans follow the team to White Hart Lane to watch their team gain a 3-0 victory against Tottenham Hotspur in the 4th round of the FA Cup. This was followed by 20,000 faithful fans who journeyed to a semi-final visit to neutral ground, Hillsborough, Sheffield, to watch a goal-less draw against Blackburn. They then returned for the replay—evidence of amazing support. The fans were rewarded with the win that took them back to Wembley, where they disposed of Arsenal 1-0. A hat-trick of 1950s Wembley wins was achieved in 1955 when Newcastle won the cup in convincing style with a 3-1 win against Manchester City. The fans of the 1950s witnessed incredible successes on the field with the silverware to match it—a feat of greatness never repeated again, to date, in the club's history.

As well as the faithful fans supporting them all the way to Wembley, one of the highlights for the players in each final was meeting with some of the most important people in the country. Members of the Royal Family, together with top military and political personnel, attended and presented the Cup and medals to winners and losers. The players were introduced one-by-one to the nobility of our country. In the 1951 Final, King George V1 attended, despite obvious illness. In 1952, that great man, Sir Winston Churchill, presented the cup to the victorious captain, Joe Harvey. What a moment that must have been for Joe. The great Jackie Milburn actually recalls Mr Churchill chatting to him before kick-off and asking if he intended grabbing the football headlines again. Sir Winston certainly knew his football and Jackie Milburn was really impressed at his football knowledge. In 1955, the young Queen Elizabeth II, with her husband Prince Philip in close attendance, presented the Cup to captain Jimmy Scoular—the stuff that dreams are made of for players and fans alike.

Fans on their way to SJP in 1956 – with Strawberry Pub in background

Chapter 3

Swinging Sixties and European Glory

The swinging sixties gave Newcastle supporters plenty to sing and dance about—a promotion to the top flight in 1965/66, and a first ever European trophy. Joe Harvey was the manager when the team were promoted at the end of the 1964/65 season as Champions of the division, and he fashioned a team of champions. They used a squad of only 14 regular players to achieve promotion. Another 6 players were involved, but each of those played less than 10 games each, but nevertheless played an important part in the promotion.

During the 1968/69 season, Newcastle United set off on an adventure that would give the supporters a flavour of playing in Europe, and extend their support farther afield to capital cities in different countries. Qualifying for the Inter-Cities Fairs Cup by virtue of the 'back door' after a 10th place finish in the league, Newcastle United marched around the continent like they owned it, and reminded Europe why Hadrian had the Geordies build his wall. Ironically, it was a Scot and a centre-back and captain of the team, Bobby Moncur, who scored three very rare career goals over a two legged final against Ujpest Dozsa. The fans had traversed the continent from Holland to Hungary, Spain to Scotland, and the football matched the carnival atmospheres the fans provided, following their beloved team both at home and overseas. The Newcastle United Supporters Club, operated directly by the club, organised a trip to Hungary for the fans. Around 200 fans made the trip, which took some organising as travel visas and flights from London to Budapest had to be arranged. The first half saw the team go 2-0 down, but a half-time team talk by Joe Harvey invigorated the team and they ran out 3-2 winners on the night, with young winger Alan Foggon scoring the winner. Having won the first leg 3-0, Newcastle United's first foray into Europe saw them winning the cup with a comfortable 6-2 aggregate win. The fans were delirious and the now famous chants of songs such as 'Noel, Noel, Noel, Noel, Wyn is the King of Newcassell.....' rang out across the stadium. Renditions of 'Frank Clark knew my Father....' and of course the sound of the 'Blaydon Races' were favourites of the fans in those heady days. The team returned to a rapturous welcome and thousands lined the streets to watch their all- conquering heroes. Stuff that dreams are made of for captain Bobby Moncur and his team.

Fairs Cup squad relax in Budapest before the final.

Having won the competition at their first attempt, they defended their cup the following season - leading to more memorable trips for fans to the likes of Anderlecht in Belgium -before being knocked out of the competition. Like a lot of good things in life, Newcastle United's Fairs Cup win of 1968/69 came like a bolt from the blue, never to be repeated. A dedicated group of fans who were swept off their feet by the marvellous achievement—'The Fairs Club'—celebrate it to this day. The Club was formed when Magpies fan Bill Gibbs had the idea of celebrating, with the players, 40 years since the Fairs Cup win. One-by-one, Bill and his pals managed to contact each player from the Fairs Cup squad. An anniversary dinner was arranged and all the players attended a truly memorable evening for both players and fans alike. Bob Moncur and Alan Foggon even travelled to Barcelona to borrow the Fairs Cup trophy, which was a magnificent gesture. Bill and his fellow fans were delighted. Since then, annual events have been organised and many players attend, even ones who played in the 1970s including the likes of Tony Green and Iam McFaul. Bill was determined that Joe Harvey, the cup winning captain of the FA Cup in 1951 and 1952 (and of course who also managed the Fairs Cup winning team) should be remembered forever at St James' Park. Along with his fellow club members and, in particular, Fairs Club Secretary Harry Watson, Bill managed to raise £10,000 for a bronze plaque in honour of Joe

Alan Foggon in the pool before the final, watched by Joe Harvey

Harvey. The London branch of Newcastle supporters, which was founded in 1964, also donated £2,500 towards the cost of the plaque—a magnificent effort by them. Newcastle United too were extremely helpful in arranging the event. The club put on a special day to celebrate the unveiling ceremony. John McNamee's son, gifted artist John junior, drew the images that were used in the making of the bronze plaque. Veteran cup winner of the 1950s, Vic Keeble, along with Bob Moncur and Joe Harvey's son, Ken, unveiled the 5ft x 3ft bronze plaque at St James' Park in March 2014. An absolutely magnificent effort by Bill, Harry and their friends in the Fairs Club made it all possible, and events are still held on an annual basis to honour the cup-winning team. It is an amazing example of a wonderful bond between players and fans that lasts even to this day, and that will stay forever in their memories.

Harry Watson and Bill Gibbs with Joe Harvey plaque

Chapter 4

1970s—Heroes and Villains down Wembley Way

The 1970s saw the arrival of a new superhero on Tyneside—Malcolm Macdonald - who was quickly named 'Supermac' by the fans. He arrived at St James' Park in true heroic style—smoking a magnificent cigar and arriving in an even more magnificent limousine. He promised to score goals and he did just that. Dashing and daring, fast and ferociously direct, he scored a hat-trick on his unforgettable debut against the mighty Liverpool at St James' Park. The fans adored him as soon as he pulled on the famous black and white stripes and he became a legend on Tyneside. Wearing the famous number 9 shirt, 'Supermac' rattled in 95 goals in 187 games and fired the Magpies to Wembley twice in the 1970s. Recognised by England, he even scored five goals in one game against Cyprus, which silenced any remaining critics who maybe felt he was not of England class.

Two Wembley finals were to follow in 1974 and 1976. However, in 1972 Newcastle United's fans had to suffer probably their biggest humiliation ever when the team were drawn away to non-league Hereford United in the FA Cup. Ronnie Radford's fabled goal—which is still shown on TV every time FA Cup games are played - made it an agonising trip home for supporters. Peter Ratcliffe, who was later to become a founder member of the Magpie Group (along with Sir John Hall) and organised away trips for fans recalls "We had drawn Hereford at home in the third round of the FA Cup in

January 1972. They were a non-league team playing in the Southern League Premier Division and they took the lead after only 17 seconds and managed to eventually hang on for a 2-2 draw which took the replay to Hereford. It was big news that the minnows had managed to avoid defeat against the mighty Newcastle United, but worse was to follow. In those days I used to organise away trips for fans and we always had full buses on the trips. We travelled with Moordale Coaches, who also transported the team to games and sometimes we would find ourselves travelling in one of the 'team buses' which were specially designed for the players, and they had a few of them. The replay was cancelled initially, due to bad weather but at last came the fateful day on 5th February 1972 when, despite the pitch wallowing in a sea of mud, the officials decided the game could go ahead. We had set off for Herefordshire in the coach full of the usual optimism and high spirits, and, despite the weather, which had caused widespread flooding in various parts of the country, we were happy to travel the many miles to cheer on our team. It was a nightmare journey but we made it through but Hereford broke our hearts and it still hurts to this day. The journey home was the longest and saddest I can recall from an away game. We arrived back on Tyneside around 3am in the early morning, rain still lashing down". An extra-time goal by Ricky George won the game for the non-league team and history was made that day.

Despite the humiliation, the fans got behind the team for the trip to face Manchester United the following week at Old Trafford. It is testament to the fans that, after such a gruelling trip to Hereford, the away trip buses were full of fans ready to cheer their team. They were not disappointed this time. It is part of the magic of being a football fan that you can be inconsolable in defeat one week then be deliriously happy the next, by tasting victory against one of the best teams in the land. A 2-0 win including a great headed goal by John Tudor, saw the fans leave Old Trafford with a victory that no Newcastle fan could have dared expect. Pride was partially restored for players and fans alike, but the wounds of the previous defeat would be difficult to heal.

In 1974, the Geordies streamed to Wembley in their thousands to watch their team be beaten soundly by Liverpool. The 3-0 defeat was a bitter pill to swallow, mainly due to the manner of defeat. Almost from the first whistle it was an uphill struggle for a strangely out-of-form Newcastle team. The dream was over once more and the fans faced bitter disappointment on the long journey back to Tyneside. As always, though, the fans kept the faith and in February 1976, a record Cup crowd of 52,760, braved a bitterly cold night at St James' Park to witness a 0-0 draw against Bolton Wanderers in the League Cup 5th round replay. A second replay saw the Magpies win 2-1, and on their way to Wembley and the League Cup Final. 30,000 Newcastle fans descended on the capital and never doubted that their team would give them the glory they craved. Sadly, a flu epidemic struck the team's preparations and, although Alan Gowling equalised an early Peter Barnes goal, a world-class bicycle kick from ex- Sunderland player Dennis Tueart won the game for City—and the Newcastle fans trudged back to Tyneside, dreams of glory well and truly shattered, once more.

Fans cheer the Magpies at Wembley 1974

There was however other Silverware up for grabs and the fans had at least some 'cups of cheer' as they saw their team win the 'Texaco Cup' twice running, in 1974 and 1975. This was a competition for clubs in England, Scotland, Northern Ireland and the Republic of Ireland who had not made it into European competitions. It was sponsored by the American Petroleum giants, Texaco, and later became known as the 'Anglo Scottish Cup' when Texaco withdrew sponsorship from 1975/76. It did not have quite the magic of the FA Cup, but the fans enjoyed the rivalry with the other fans from the home nations.

In the Summer of 1976, Malcolm 'Supermac' Macdonald was sold to Arsenal for the rather unusual fee of £333,333. The fans had lost their goal-scoring machine and it would be quite a few years before there was a replacement good enough to grace the number 9 shirt left vacant by him. Worse was to follow for the fans, as the club were relegated to the Second Division at the end of the 1977/78 season. Average attendances for the next few seasons fell to around the 25,000 mark. Yet, they were still one of the best supported teams outside of the First Division and, by far, the best supported team in the lower division. The fans still travelled the country in search of glory with their team.

Newcastle fans at Wembley, 1976

Chapter 5

1980s and Keegan Mania

A 3-1 New Year's Day win at St James' Park over Sunderland on the first day of the 1980s was a good omen for the new decade. Yet, it would take two years before long-suffering Newcastle fans had something to celebrate on the new animated scoreboard. This was the arrival of King Kev, The Messiah, The Pied Piper. Few men, if any, in Newcastle's long history had the effect Kevin Keegan did on Newcastle United and no-one has ever tapped into the power and love of the fans so much.

'KeeganMania' part one whipped Tyneside into a frenzy when the England Captain swapped the South Coast and First Division top-flight football with Southampton, for a promotion push in the old Second Division in 1982 with the Magpies. Keegan was as impressed with the Newcastle fans as much as they were with him, saying: "They are far and away the best supporters in the land. I've enjoyed the roars of the Liverpool Kop but i've never heard anything like today".

He scored on his Magpies debut against Queens Park Rangers as almost 36,000 fans packed into St James' Park on 28th August 1982. It was a game destined to pass into Newcastle United folklore. Alan Shearer revealed recently on a Barclays 'Spirit of the Game' advert that Keegan's debut was the very first game he attended as a fan and which became the inspiration for his fabulous football career. He recalls:

"We decided to go the night before ... we took the Metro first thing ... I had to get a scarf ... I can't believe my dad kept it all these years ... I remember we bought a pie ... We got there early, we weren't the only ones ... I'll never forget how it felt entering the Gallowgate for the first time ... .or getting lifted in the air when we scored ... The atmosphere, the feeling, the adulation ... it was then I knew I HAD to be a footballer ..."

Kevin Keegan bids farewell after his final league game, May 1984

Newcastle had lift off and - after two memorable seasons, including one with a thrilling forward line of Keegan, Beardsley and Waddle, who scored 65 goals between them in 1983/84 - promotion was secured. Keegan's impact was felt as much off the pitch as on it. He galvanised the fans and all of Tyneside to believe that their beloved club could really go places once again. Thousands of fans followed a Keegan-inspired team around the country, often boosting away crowds by up to 10,000 and filling St James' Park to almost full capacity—sometimes achieving the distinction of hosting the highest home crowd in the country, despite their Second Division status. The fans loved every minute. Graham Wallis, who runs his Newcastle United-themed Barber Shop in Shiremoor, Newcastle upon Tyne, recalls the most exciting time for him as a fan was the 1980s. Graham hasn't missed a game for more than 30 years and Newcastle fans call into his shop for a haircut and a team talk. By his own admission, it's best to go when Newcastle have just won!

Graham Wallis in his Newcastle United themed Barbershop

Keegan left as dramatically as he had arrived in a helicopter after a special farewell match against Liverpool, having secured promotion as he promised to do before retiring. Alan Shearer was one of the ball boys for the game but, after this football feast, came famine and the seeds of later unrest when manager Arthur Cox left abruptly, over a row with promised transfer funds not materialising.

Three wins in the first three games rocketed Newcastle to the top of the First Division under new manager, Jack Charlton in 1984/85, but the bubble was to burst as flowing football was replaced by a more direct style and Newcastle finished in 14th place. The rest of the decade saw the team tread water, then sink, as local stars Chris Waddle and Paul Gascoigne were sold to Spurs and Peter Beardsley left for Liverpool.

The only treats Newcastle fans had enjoyed in the late 1980s were 'M & Ms'—the signing of English football's first Brazilian, Mirandinha, and trips to Wembley for the Mercantile Credit Trophy finals, but sadly no silverware for the fans to celebrate. 'Miramagic' against Liverpool and Manchester United earned a win at Anfield and a point at Old Trafford as Mirandinha dazzled in front of fans wearing sombrero hats! The other famous 'M' was Micky Quinn, a centre forward who thrilled the almost 30,000 crowd on his debut with four goals in August 1989. He became an instant hero and the crowds packed into St James' Park, as the club chased promotion under Jim Smith.

Mick Quinn recalls walking through the streets of Newcastle after being signed and seeing a group of fans known as 'The Boardbusters' carrying a banner which read 'Who the **** is Micky Quinn?'. Delighted and surprised, the fans certainly knew all about their new centre forward when the team overpowered Leeds United 5-2 on his debut. Mick's four-goal haul is still talked about on Tyneside some 25 years after the game. Fan revolution was afoot, however, and 'The Magpie Group' swooped in. The group was formerly known as NSA (Newcastle Supporters Association) and was born out of a chance meeting between Malcolm Dix and John Hall (now Sir John Hall) in the early 1980s. John Hall had been approached by Newcastle United regarding club sponsorship, and Malcolm invited John to the next AGM of the club. John told the club he would consider investing in the club, but was concerned over the sales of Beardsley, Waddle and Gascoigne. Multi-millionaire businessman Hall met up with journalist Bob Cass, and together produced an article which appeared in the Mail on Sunday and that cited the case for a takeover of the club. John Gibson, from the Newcastle Evening Chronicle, organised a meeting with his Editor Graeme Stanton and, together with John Hall and his son Douglas, agreed to approach well-known local characters who had funds available to become members of the Magpie Group. Local Newcastle businessmen such as Joe Robertson, Bobby Pattinson, Brian Reed and David Stephenson all became members of the group. Other previous NSA members, including John Waugh and Peter Ratcliffe, were brought on board to help persuade current shareholders to sell their shares and a big launch was held. There were certainly some boardroom battles! Malcolm Dix had shares passed down through his family and, eventually, John Hall became major shareholder when Gavin Westwood finally sold his substantial family shareholding in the club. After a long and bitter battle, John Hall became club Chairman in 1992 and a new era of excitement for the fans was just around the corner—with the return of Kevin Keegan, this time as manager.

Animated St James' Park scoreboard, 1980s

Chapter 6

The Fans—The Pride and The Passion

Some folk are born into supporting Newcastle United and some fall in love with the team in their teenage years or even as adults. This chapter is the first of several dedicated to some of those fans whose support for their team wears deep into the fabric of their everyday lives. Michael Chaplin, Durham-born writer and TV Producer, is one such fan, and his love of football has influenced his literary work. His play *Hope, Beautiful Game* which was produced for Newcastle Live Theatre, was an exploration of the history and culture of football on Tyneside. This is Michael's story.

"It all began with that noise.

I moved to Newcastle with my family in 1957, to live on the edge of Jesmond Vale. One of my earliest memories of the house is of playing with my new friend, Charlie (he's still my best mate by the way) on the steps by the front door. Suddenly, we heard this tremendous noise in the distance, a wild cheering rolling over the rooftops from the centre of town. I didn't know what it was but Charlie had heard it before. 'It's the crowd at St James's,' he said. 'Newcastle must have scored.' In that instant, I knew I wanted to hear that sound close-up and be a part of that baying crowd. I became a fan.

It was a while before I actually went to a match. My father (the writer Sid Chaplin) had no interest in football, and my older brother Chris hated it, so I had no one to take me. I must have been around 11 when I plucked up the courage to go on my own, handing over my pocket money at the turnstiles and fighting my way to the front at the Popular Side to join all the other little lads. I can't remember who we played but I know we won, 1-0 I think, with a goal from a big bruiser called Ron McGarry who knee'd in a cross from the skilful Alan Suddick on the wing. For the first time, I experienced that scary but wonderful surge down the terracing by a celebrating crowd. I went home happy, but didn't tell my family—I'd have got wrong. I returned for the next home match, and countless times in the 50 years since, to what Bobby Robson called 'the cathedral of football on the hill'. Not an inappropriate analogy - for years and years before her death my mother would ask me: 'Are you going to pray this Saturday?'

Michael Chaplin

For some years now, since I returned from exile in London, I've had a season ticket, sitting next to my friend and collaborator, Max Roberts, the artistic director of Live Theatre, with whom I've created three stage plays about the history, culture and politics of Newcastle United. (Who knows—there might be another one of these days!) Often, in my London years, I'd get the train up from King's Cross for a match, savouring the prospects of the afternoon ahead, often crawling home again in three hours of brooding disappointment But I also trawled around all the grounds in the South-East to stand in the away end, often in misery, the worst experience being a 4-1 defeat at Southend one Boxing Day just before the Second Coming of the Blessed Kevin.

In all these years I've seen some fabulous players (and, of course, some real duds), but if I had to plump for one of the former, it would have to be Peter Beardsley—so clever and deft, and such speed of thought and execution, and a local lad too. As for the latter, there are perhaps too many to mention, but there is always one Marcelino, whose sorry exploits on the pitch were in such stark contrast to his glittering name. I've seen some marvellous matches too: the 4-0 drubbing of Feyenoord in our first European tie in the Fairs Cup-winning run; the famous 'Howay 5-0' against Man United, standing in disbelief in a London boozer packed with sick blokes in red; a 5-0 thumping of Carlisle that confirmed our promotion back in 1984, also memorable for the fact that it was the first time I'd taken my two sons, the youngest Tom then only 7, thus cementing the loyalty of these two London boys to their Dad's hometown team (sorry lads, I know you could have been Chelsea fans); and spinning the wheel forward a generation, taking my grandson Ollie to the marvellous 3-2 defeat of Chelsea in the 2012/13 season at St James' Park.

That, in a nutshell is my football story. My commitment to Newcastle United was an important part of becoming a Tynesider all those years ago and it's been a life sentence, in more ways than one. But I can't do anything about it: it's part of who and what I am and now passed on to the generations below. I realise there probably won't be any rewards in terms of silverware soon—can any Newcastle fan honestly state his or her conviction that we are about to end the glory drought?—but I'm not going anywhere else. I am, as my mother used to say, plain black-and-white daft ..."

Val McLane is a well known local actress, writer and teacher. In 1973 Val was a co-founder of 'Live Theatre' which created plays and stories that were relevant to the North East community. The company has gone from strength to strength over the years and these days is based on the Quayside in Newcastle and helps develop new writing talent in the region.

Val is an enthusiastic fan and told us : "I became interested in football in my teens and went to a number of Newcastle matches with my pal, Rosie, and we liked to watch George Eastham. I met a trainee footballer, Martin McLane, when I was sixteen years old and married him six years later. After we married, we discovered that we both had great uncles who played for Newcastle United in the 1920s. They were actually in the same team photo!

Val McLane

My relative was Eddie Mooney and Martin's was Sandy Mutch. Eddie won a cup medal and played 22 times for Newcastle. He played in midfield. Sandy was a goalkeeper and made 15 appearances for the club.

I once met Paul Gascoigne at a function when he was a popular young player and asked him what he did for a living. Everyone else knew who he was except me but I wished him well and said I hoped he'd be successful. I've met other players since then and Peter Beardsley always speaks to me when we bump into each other. As a family we have supported Newcastle United through thick and thin and will continue to do so".

Chapter 7

1990s and the Return of the Messiah

The early 1990s were the calm before the storm. A bitter loss in a two-legged promotion play-off to Sunderland, a side who had finished sixth to Newcastle's third, ended in unsavoury scenes as some very emotional fans invaded the pitch. Yet, it ultimately proved to be the precursor to brighter times ahead. United fan John Morgan recollects trips to St James' Park in the early 1990s:

"I got a fiver pocket money and it was 20p return on the bus to town and £3.50 to get into the match. There was just enough left to buy a match programme and a Magpies chocolate bar at half-time. My pals and I would be first ones in the ground. We were in the Milburn paddock and making sure we got the best positions behind the dugout and tunnel to get autographs from the players. Mind you, we used to get well squashed when the ground filled up and Newcastle scored! Once Keegan came as manager in 1992, the whole atmosphere changed . . ."

If the 'Scoreboard' had been the area for the hardcore faithful to congregate and sing in the 1980s, then its rival took over in the 1990s—'The Corner', as it was known. They had plenty to sing about when the Messiah returned. Nearly a decade after Keegan had transformed the club as a player, he repeated the trick as manager. He rescued the club from the jaws of relegation to

Division 3 in 1991/92 and won promotion to the newly styled Premiership, playing superbly entertaining football—manna from heaven for the Geordie faithful. Keegan instinctively understood the Newcastle fans. He advised his players: "Have time for the fans and they will have time for you". Then he set about delivering what the fans wanted on an unprecedented scale. Over the next five years, the Toon Roller Coaster was set firmly on course for the stars as the second coming of the Messiah heralded title challenges with Sir Alex Ferguson's Manchester United and a startling return to European football. A 5-0 away win in Antwerp after an absence of 16 years had fans singing and dancing in the streets and loving every minute of 'The Entertainers'.

Fans having fun in Monaco, UEFA Cup Quarter-Final 1997

Keegan-Mania part 2 meant attendances shot up to such an extent that the stadium was extended to cope with the increased demand. Initially, its capacity swelled to around 36,000 and then, in 2001, to the present capacity of over 50,000. There were regular rumours of moving to a new stadium on the Town Moor or, heaven forbid, across the Tyne to Gateshead. The waiting lists for season tickets were, at times, 10,000 strong as entry to the Gallowgate became as rare as a golden ticket to Willy Wonka's Chocolate Factory. The marvellous feast of football on display inside the ground was equally spectacular. Peter Beardsley was, again, instrumental as he arrived back from Everton for his second spell as a player with the club. Marvellous British talents such as Rob Lee, Andy Cole and Les Ferdinand—along with a galaxy of international stars such as Philippe Albert, David Ginola and the magical Faustino Asprilla—shot Newcastle and their fans back to prominence. So sky-high was the optimism under Keegan, the fans' expectations rose to new heights. St James' Park had become a fortress and, for most games, pre-match talk was about by how many the team would win, rather than expecting to ever lose a game. Newcastle beat Leicester on the final day of the promotion season and they would sweep 4, 5 and 6 goals against very good teams on their way to the Premiership. They even achieved seventh heaven for the fans against Notts County, in the League Cup and both Swindon and Spurs in the Premier League the following year. The Magpies became the nation's 'second team' with everyone willing them to beat Fergie's men to the

Down Wembley Way - 1998 FA Cup Final v Arsenal

title. Huge crowds of fans even turned up regularly in big numbers to watch the players train at unique open training sessions, with attendances reaching the thousands at some sessions.

After a near-miss title bid in 1995/96, the £15 million world-record signing of local lad Alan Shearer had the fans in raptures once more. Sadly, Keegan left in controversial circumstances not long afterwards, but his relationship with the fans had mainly been second-to-none. The only time the fans were really unhappy were when some of them confronted Keegan on the steps of St James' following the sale of Andy Cole to Manchester United in 1994. He fully understood the fans' frustration. Some of his comments at the time were as follows: "We had an open board meeting with the fans. . . People sometimes think fans don't know what the game is all about . . . They know more than sometimes people in the club know . . . You look at them and they put things on forums or in papers and you think, wow, how could he know? . . . that's exactly what I think . . . how would he know that?" For the remainder of the decade, Newcastle fans had two trips to Wembley under Kenny Dalglish and Ruud Gullit, which sadly produced no silverware. It was the semi-final games that live longer in the memory for many fans. Almost 25,000 fans took over Old Trafford against Spurs. Their deafening noise shook the foundations of the stadium when Duncan Fer-

Lone Ranger, 'Toonto' and The Pope, Wembley 1999

guson warmed up on the touchline and Shearer smashed in his goals. One of the security guards admitted he had never experienced such volume or atmosphere at any game at Old Trafford that he could remember.

Ant and Dec, Wembley 1999

Nicola Wintrip was among the fans who travelled to Wembley to watch the 1999 FA Cup Final against Man United. Some fans turned up in all manner of fancy dress—which included a possee of 'Elvis' lookalikes, The 'Lone Ranger and Toonto' and even one fan dressed as the Pope! Added to that weird and wonderful collection of characters, she found herself sitting near such well known faces as 'Sting', Jimmy Nail and Ant and Dec. Nicola has kindly let us use her photos which accompany this chapter. She has been attending games since the 1987/88 season and has travelled to more than 100 grounds to follow the team. She is looking forward to adding Bournemouth to that impressive collection in 2015/16. She recalls a harrowing trip to war-torn Sarajevo, involving a NATO helicopter escort, and more pleasant jaunts to the San Siro and the Nou Camp. There has been as much pain as pleasure on her adventures. She ended up for the third time at Wembley in the back of a St John Ambulance—twice for dehydration and the third time for injuries picked up in the mad celebrations following Rob Lee's goal in the semi-final against Chelsea. Meeting Sir Bobby Robson in Sarajevo, before the game against Zeljeznicar, is her most treasured Magpie moment.

'Sting' at Wembley 1999

NUFC 'Elvises' at Wembley 1999

It is often said that if Newcastle had a team to match the passion of their fans, they would win everything in sight. In the 1990s, the fans had a team of which they could be proud. More importantly, the team had magnificent fans to be proud of, too.

Jimmy Nail at Wembley 1999

Chapter 8

Fans Rivalry: Across the Divide

The rivalry between Newcastle and Sunderland fans has been well documented for decades. For many, feelings have ran very high each and every season the teams have played in the same league. One football expert has been uniquely placed between the two sides—Doug Weatherall, a Daily Mail reporter for more than fifty years. Doug has an uncanny allegiance with both clubs and he has kindly shared his first-hand experiences as a journalist and a neutral fan of North East football.

"It's still the question I'm asked most. Even 56 years after first reporting North-East Football, fans around Tyne, Wear and Tees still wonder which team I support and there's still widespread disbelief when I say 'All of Them'. Not convinced? Well, to underline my point, let me explain that before Newcastle met Sunderland in March 2012 at St James' Park (yes, I know all about that other name!), I wanted Newcastle to take the points. Reason: Newcastle needed them the more for possible qualification for European action whereas Sunderland, while virtually safe from relegation, still had a chance of winning the FA Cup. It was a pleasant change. Too often in my time points were needed for league safety and whichever club was the more threatened had my backing. Such thinking has also applied over the years when Newcastle and Sunderland have met Middlesbrough. Remarkably, people who didn't really know me have always thought I didn't back their favourites. Geordie fans, for example, reckoned I was a Mackem or Boro man. Yet, it's many years ago I illustrated my lack of bias with an April 1st radio broadcast. I set an exciting scene: Newcastle United vs. Sunderland in a European Cup final. Realising listeners would want to know whom I'd wish to win this dream fixture, I revealed: 'The team I believed would have the better chance of retaining the trophy the following season'. A chance would be a fine thing . . .

Doug & Journalists with Joe Harvey, prior to Fairs Cup Final 1969 (Doug is front row, middle)

I wasn't always 'neutral'. Even though this book is very much Newcastle United focused, I should stress—or, should I say, confess—I supported Sunderland from boyhood. Born in Seaham, County Durham, in the cup-winning year of 1932 for Newcastle United, I have an abiding first football memory of my dad returning from a first London trip with a toy sword for me. He'd seen Sunderland beat Preston North End 3-1 at Wembley. So I treasured my first book, The Inside Story of Football by George Allison, Arsenal's County Durham-born manager. Its pictures included that of my boyhood idol, Raich Carter, holding the Cup while chaired by team-mates. I wasn't to know that, through journalism, Raich would become a good friend of mine. Neither could I have imagined I'd become close to some of the greatest names in Newcastle United's history, like 'Wor Jackie' Milburn and Bobby Mitchell. Picture me as a 19-year-old National Service soldier in Austria in 1952. I am in Klagenfurt Gashaus with lads from all over the North East, celebrating Newcastle's retention of the FA Cup by beating Arsenal with a George Robledo goal. My army job was then editing a command weekly newspaper, having started work before call-up as a 16-year-old general news reporter with the Sunderland Echo.

No one could have had a more enjoyable career. I've loved it. If there was a minus, it was that work prevented me from continuing to play football or cricket on Saturdays. I'd kept goal in the most successful under-14's school team, Ryhope Grammar, the North East has ever known. While playing for Dawdon Colliery Welfare Juniors, I had the chance of a trial with Norwich City. That was after an evening cup-final win, but that very day I'd accepted an offer to join the Echo when I left school. So, I played midweek football and captained Seaham Harbour's third team at cricket. I also enjoyed both sports as a soldier and, again in midweek, as a Manchester-based reporter with the Daily Herald. While delighting in the variety of news coverage, I was persuaded to give Newcastle-based sports work a go. The six-month trial has stretched quite a bit . . . Highlights? Obviously, Newcastle's Joe Harvey-led winning of the Inter Cities Fairs Cup in 1969 and Sunderland's 1973 fairy-tale FA Cup win. Joe Harvey's best man, 1955 Magpies Cup winner Bob Stokoe, was their 'Messiah'.

My personal stamp on football history was a piece I wrote for the Daily Mail in 1967. Short of a topical subject for a weekly offbeat column, the granting of a Charlie Hurley testimonial at Roker Park got me round to thinking of stars who'd been similarly honoured: the likes of Sir Stanley Matthews, Sir

Tom Finney and Nat Lofthouse. Thus, the name of a Newcastle great came to mind—'Wor Jackie'. Ten years after he left Newcastle United, I wrote that he should have a testimonial. Jackie couldn't believe it when his wife Laura showed him the article. My telephone conversation with Chairman Lord Westwood, on the day my piece appeared, convinced me there was little chance of Board co-operation. The Chairman questioned, indeed, whether such a match would attract a crowd. 'Oh, yes'! I replied. I was determined that wouldn't be the end of things and immediately rang Bill McEwen, the Chairman of Newcastle Supporters' Club. He enthused about my suggestion that his committee should seek permission to stage a Milburn match, and when I reported they'd do just that, I knew the Board would agree. Saying no when such an idol was involved would have been a more controversial story than their yes. The Milburn night was wonderful. It rained all day but, even though it wasn't an all-ticket occasion, it attracted the North East's then biggest testimonial crowd. Not long afterwards, I was puzzled when I noticed a brown paper parcel on a seat of my car outside my Gosforth home. In it was a sliver plaque with the inscription 'St James' Park. Attendance 46,000. To Doug with everlasting gratitude for your journalistic approach in starting my testimonial match. 10th May 1967'. And there at the centre, in gold handwriting, was the name, Jack Milburn. To say I was moved and proud would be an understatement. The heirloom is treasured in

Doug & Brian Clough, Majorca 1974, chasing the story of Cloughie's switch to manage Leeds Utd.

the Weatherall household. I was proud, too, when the Milburn family asked me to give the eulogy at another memorable occasion, Jackie's funeral service at St Nicholas' Cathedral, Newcastle.

As a veteran observer of North East football, I've since eulogised at the funerals of Bobby Mitchell (a wonderful friend and my favourite all-time Newcastle player); the third Newcastle three-times Cup winner, Bobby Cowell; Bob Stokoe; former Bradford, Burnley, Sunderland and England winger, Billy Elliott; and Ian Porterfield, scorer of Sunderland's Wembley winner in 1973. It's said in journalism that names make news. These and many others have helped make my life a joy".

Doug has experienced life as a fan on both sides of the divide and it is a poignant reminder that, whatever team we support, we can still enjoy respect and healthy rivalry in equal measure. That is certainly the best we can hope to achieve when the tempo is at fever pitch to win the bragging rights each season, whether your stripes are black-and-white or red-and-white.

Doug with treasured silver plaque

Chapter 9

On The Pitch and Singing our Praises!

Every club has some well-known fans and Newcastle United have plenty of their own to sing about. Some of our greatest North-East actors, musicians and TV stars are dedicated followers, and when time allows they watch their beloved team in action. One such colourful character is Graeme Danby, a local lad with a fabulous singing voice, who works with English National Opera and performs regularly at the Royal Opera House, Covent Garden. He was more than happy to talk about his love for Newcastle United. Despite being on tour for much of the time, he still manages to watch the team whenever time and travel allows. Graeme attended his first match at St James' Park when he was just seven-months-old, along with his dad, and has been attending as many games as possible ever since. Graeme's most memorable game was in 2002 when Newcastle United played Sheffield United at Old Trafford in the FA Cup. He took his wife to the game for the first time and Graeme was keen for her to experience the drama and passion of watching the team in action. When Alan Shearer scored the goal to give his team victory, he wanted to share the moment with Valerie, only to realise that fellow fans had hoisted her into the air in celebration of the goal. Another game that Graeme particularly remembers was at Upton Park in 2005 when he went to see Newcastle United play the Hammers. He was with politician Michael McManus, who is an avid West Ham fan, and they sat with 'the troops' and Graeme was in full voice singing along with the fans.

Newcastle won the game 2-0 but Graeme lost his voice that day with too much chanting. This was most unfortunate as he was rehearsing for 'La Traviata' at the time. Luckily, his voice returned just in time for the show but, from then on, wife Valerie banned him from singing on the terraces at future games.

Graeme Danby entertains the fans at St James'

When Chris Mort was brought as Club Chairman in 2007, he was desperate to improve the atmosphere that had become rather subdued due to the lack of success on the pitch. He approached Graeme with a proposition—asking him if he would entertain the Geordie fans prior to kick-off at the big derby game versus Sunderland. Graeme was actually rehearsing in Milan at that time. However, the club were so keen for his services, they flew him by private plane especially for the game. Graeme strolled onto the pitch wearing a Newcastle United shirt and sang the first three verses of 'Blaydon Races'. The fans absolutely loved it and Graeme recalls the noise and applause was almost deafening. When he chanted 'Toon Toon' afterwards, the crowds were delirious! He had exactly two minutes and thirty six seconds in which to sing the song before kick-off, which he admits was not easy as it is a science to be able to do that as he had to slow it right down. The fans loved it and Graeme became an instant hero of the terraces. On another occasion, Graeme was invited to sing live at Gosforth Park Racecourse when Channel 4 were in attendance. He also sang the same song at Peter Beardsley's testimonial Dinner, albeit using different words, in tribute to a player he has always believed is one of our unsung heroes.

The most poignant football event for Graeme was when he was asked to perform at the 'Night of Three Knights'—a tribute to Sir Bobby Robson, Sir Bobby Charlton and Sir Alex Ferguson at Rainton Meadows in Durham. Graeme sang a North-East favourite song, 'I'm Gonna Leave Old Durham Town', especially for Sir Bobby—by way of a duet with Mick Hucknall of the top band Simply Red. Afterwards, Graeme made a point of mentioning that on this particular occasion, only one of the duo sang live and it wasn't Mick Hucknall! The event raised more than £100,000 for charity and Graeme has fond memories of sharing a breakfast table with Sir Bobby Charlton the following morning.

Pals together - Alan Shearer and Graeme Danby

Although Graeme lives in the South these days, his feeling for his football club and his hometown is never far from his heart. So much so, he has officially registered the name of his home as 'Toon Towers'. A black-and-white supporter through and through.

Graeme on stage at La Scala Opera House, Milan

Chapter 10

A New Decade—2000 and beyond

Sir Bobby Robson took over the reins at Newcastle when Ruud Gullit was sacked in September 1999, and the great Geordie Knight presided over a fabulous new era when his teams achieved three consecutive top five finishes, as well as some European adventures thrown in. Robson was the overwhelmingly popular choice—the fans' favourite. The club secured their manager at the second attempt after a near miss in 1997, when his honouring of a contract at Barcelona meant the dream choice of Keegan replacement never materialised. Many have speculated over the years what would have happened if Bobby Robson had inherited Keegan's full complement of Entertainers in 1997. Yet it was a case of 'better late than never' when the delirious faithful were treated to a feast of goals on Robson's home debut with an 8-0 win against Sheffield Wednesday. Alan Shearer bagged five of the goals. The fans were resurgent once more after the dark days of Gullit and the Robson revolution was kick-started on September 19th, 1999. By the following April, Robson had Newcastle back at Wembley for a semi-final against Chelsea and many fans we spoke to consider the moment Robert Lee scored from an Alan Shearer cross, to equalise Gus Poyet's early strike, as one of their favourite goals. Long-time fan and East Stand season ticket holder Dick Fenn remembers: "It was total carnage when Rob Lee scored. We ended up seven rows in front of where we were sitting at Wembley. Absolute mayhem". Sadly, a late Poyet winner dashed Newcastle's hopes and it was no fairytale trip home to Tyneside for the disappointed fans.

Within two years, though, Newcastle fans were in heaven once more as their team were back at football's top table—The Champions League. In 2001, players such as Laurent Robert brought some much-needed Gallic flair to the team. The sheer pace of striker Craig Bellamy, together with the goals of Shearer, made St James' Park an exciting place to be for the Geordie faithful and the team hovered in the upper reaches of the top division. A year on, and a last-gasp goal from Bellamy scraped Newcastle a win against Feyenoord and into the heady heights of the Champions League Second Phase. This set up mouth-watering clashes with the likes of Barcelona and Inter Milan and created unforgettable memories and overseas trips for the fans. Four thousand Geordies made the trip to Catalonia in December 2002, yet only 2,000 actually made it into the Nou Camp for the game after it was delayed for one night due to torrential rain. "We're supposed to be at home!" was the chant of those able to postpone flights and their return to work. Instead, they experienced two magical nights in Barcelona. The rain certainly did not dampen their spirits or their enthusiasm one bit. Although the team were valiant in defeat, the fans were disappointed not to gain a famous victory. Sir Bobby paid special tribute to the travelling fans: "I'd like to thank them very much for sticking with us. I would think that it's cost a little bit more money for some of them—they were probably due to return yesterday but didn't. They stayed in Catalonia and they've enjoyed it, and I hope we can give them something back in the next four games. They were wonderful. I wouldn't swap them for anybody".

Another trip to the San Siro saw 12,000 Geordies stream into the stadium to witness their team take the lead twice against Internazionale through Alan Shearer. It was an unforgettable night for the fans. In the words of the legendary 'Biffa' of NUFC.com: "The ball gets dispatched from Robert into the box and somehow Big Al is there to knock it home. The carnival has started again and there's Gosforth's favourite son in front of us, arms aloft, with a Peruvian climbing on his shoulders, as thousand of Geordies go collectively nuts. He's scored. For Newcastle. Against Inter. In Milan. And we're there—and we're winning. '2-1 in the San Siro' was the song —Manna for the ears. Bloody Hell!'.

At that stage, those Newcastle fans present wouldn't have swapped their place on this earth and alongside this pitch for anything, anyone or anywhere: even bedroom romps with film stars, swimming in vats of vodka, or breaking the bank at Monte Carlo. Moments like that you can't buy on Ebay!

Fans pay tribute to Alan shearer at Testimonial

Sporadic European campaigns under Graeme Souness and Glenn Roeder followed Robson's controversial dismissal, yet title challenges were off the menu. Souness did lead Newcastle to an FA Cup semi-final in Cardiff in 2005 when Shola Ameobi grabbed a consolation goal against Manchester United. The 30,000-strong Geordie invasion of the Millennium Stadium were once more disappointed and the long trek home was a miserable one.

In 2006, more than 15,000 fans welcomed the arrival of the new number 9, Michael Owen. He was totally overawed by the welcome as he was introduced to the crowd in front of the Leazes End, along with his wife and children. Sadly, his career with the Magpies was plagued with injury and it was left to Alan Shearer, in his last season as a player, to provide the fans with two golden memories of the 2005/6 campaign. The first was his record-breaking 206th goal against Portsmouth at the Gallowgate End to break Jackie Milburn's all-time NUFC goal-scoring record. The rapturous chants of 'Shearer, Shearer' rang out across every side of the stadium. Almost the entire stadium was in full voice and it is doubtful if that occasion will ever be bettered at St James' Park. The second momentous memory was Shearer's final game in a Newcastle shirt, away to Sunderland. He scored a penalty with his last-ever kick in professional football to help achieve a famous victory. His smile and celebration will live long in the memory of all the Geordie fans who were lucky enough to witness the occasion.

The arrival of Mike Ashley as owner in 2007 saw 'King Kev' return for a short spell as manager but, after his departure, a period of managerial instability and boardroom unrest led to Newcastle's relegation in 2009 after a season of four managers: Kevin Keegan, Joe Kinnear, Chris Hughton and, finally, Shearer himself. After the bitter disappointment of relegation, the 'Toon Army' felt naturally despondent that summer. But, as always in football, another new dawn would break and the team would go on to bring the smiles back once more to the faces of the long-suffering Geordie faithful.

Chapter 11

Famous Faces Around the Table

It has been the author's privilege to spend time with famous and not-so-famous fans who attend St James' Park whenever they can. Many have been happy to join us at the 'Football Passion table' in the Moncur Suite at St James' Park to share with us their fond reminiscences of supporting their favourite team. Very special thanks to those who have joined us, despite very busy schedules both at home and abroad. Our table has hosted such well-known Geordie actors as Robson Green and Tim Healy, along with Tim's great friend and fellow Geordie, film director, Geoff Wonfor. Robson has been a big fan since boyhood and attends whenever possible. He is often to be seen in the Gallowgate End singing along with the fans, despite his television fishing and drama schedules playing havoc with his free time. Over the years, Robson has attended many 'away' games both in the UK and abroad and has always flown the Geordie flag wherever he happens to be in the world. Tim hasn't been able to attend as many games as he would like as he has spent a lot of time in Spain during the last few years, filming the smash-hit comedy 'Benidorm'. However, with the marvels of Sky TV, he manages to keep up-to-date with the latest goings-on at SJP. When asked his opinion on the Newcastle fans, Tim replied: "The fans are the most devoted in the whole of the UK. Wherever you go, far and wide, you meet Newcastle fans. Some are working far from home and others have moved away, but they love their team so much. I believe we have the best fans in the country—where else would you get 50,000 fans in the bad times? They are the best."

Ian Payne and Robson Green

From the world of rock we have hosted founder member of iconic band Lindisfarne, Ray Laidlaw, and the band's lead singer, Billy Mitchell. Occasionally the band's famous songs, such as 'Meet Me On The Corner' and 'Run For Home', are played in the stadium on match days. In 2014, Ray was absolutely delighted when he took his seat to the sounds of Sunset Sons, his son Jed's band, performing their hit song 'Remember'. A proud moment indeed for both father and son. Billy Mitchell recalls the 5-1 demolition of Sunderland in 2010 and the iconic 4-4 draw with Arsenal in 2011 as his most memorable matches. He actually joined our table for both of those games and, against Arsenal, had to take a bit of stick at half-time from a well-known Gunners fan, top comedian Alan Davies, who also joined us that day. Afterwards, Alan was almost speechless after Newcastle's amazing comeback from four goals down. A lot of friendly banter, some of it more than a little bit blue, was exchanged that day!

Geoff Wonfor and Tim Healy

4-0 down at half-time to Arsenal - "we just need one to make a comeback" - indicates Billy Mitchell

The North East's very first World Boxing Champion, Glenn McCrory, is an avid fan and attends games whenever his busy schedule allows. Glenn's love affair with the game began when he started playing football at the age of seven for his local school team, St Patrick's in Stanley, County Durham. When Newcastle United signed 'Supermac' Malcolm Macdonald, he felt so inspired that he decided to follow in his footsteps and scored more hat-tricks than any other player at school. He was presented with a trophy by Sir Bobby Robson. His proudest football moment came when he actually played on the coveted turf at St James' Park in a Charity Game for the Prince's Trust, some years ago. He played alongside superstars such as Alan Shearer and Paul Gascoigne. Even though he was only on the pitch for fifteen minutes or so, he had his moments of football fame proudly wearing a number 10 shirt.

Malcolm Macdonald and Glenn McCrory

'Pam and Ian', a.k.a. ITV local news presenters Pam Royle and Ian Payne, provided excellent company, too. Ian is a familiar face at St James' Park on match days and discusses the merits or otherwise of each game with ex-players and fans alike. Pam attends games whenever possible. She told us: "The club is an integral part of the city and beyond. How it performs helps to set the mood and self-esteem of our patch. It's not just fans and friends of the club that share the passion. Everybody in the city seems to have more of a bounce in their step when the club is doing well!"

Pam Royle

Jade Thirlwall, local lass and singer with top girl band 'Little Mix', also joined us and was delighted to meet the Fairs Cup winning Captain Bob Moncur in the Moncur Suite. Jade was absolutely marvellous and showed incredible love and patience with many of the young fans who wanted photos taken with her—and with older fans, too, of course! Her good friend Josef Craig, gold medal winner in the 2012

Jade Thirlwall and Bobby Moncur with Fairs Cup

Summer Paralympics in the men's 400m freestyle event, was with Jade that day. They were wonderful guests and Josef was delighted when his favourite player, goalkeeper Tim Krul, actually came to see him at the table and wanted to chat about his record-breaking swimming exploits. Jade and Josef are shining examples of young, local talent and are inspirational to younger fans. Despite very busy schedules, they do a great deal of charitable work in the area. They visit schools in their hometowns of South Shields and Jarrow and make the day of many senior citizens, when they spend time at the local care homes for elderly people.

Tim Krul and Josef Craig

Geordie entertainer Charlie Richmond also provided great company last season. He told us "My passion for football and Newcastle United began when I was very young. My first ever game at St James' Park was in the late 1980s against Wolves. My cousins Stephen and Kevin Nicolson took me to the Gallowgate End behind the goal and sat me and my other cousin, Sean, on top of the white concrete stands that folk leant against. All I can remember is one minute we were watching the game and the next minute Newcastle scored. The entire stand rushed forwards and Sean and I ended up almost on the pitch. That was my first ever memory of going to a game. These days my father and brother-in-law have seats in the 1892 section. I try to attend as many home games as possible, whenever I'm home".

Charlie Richmond

We are so blessed that we have so much talent in our region that extends beyond the football pitch!

Ray Laidlaw and signed shirt

Chapter 12

The Gates Come Home

Sir John Hall is remembered warmly by the fans as the man who brought exciting times back to the city when Newcastle nearly won the Premier League in 1995/96 with Kevin Keegan and his team of 'Entertainers'. When the original gates to the stadium were removed in 1999 due to upgrading work, they were transported to Sir John's property at Woolsington Hall. There they lay covered in grass, until one special day when they were taken back to their ancestral home—St James' Park.

'The Leazes Gates', as they were known, were intended to form the entrance to a new club training centre, following their removal from the stadium. However, planning permission was denied and the club changed hands. So the gates remained in their grassy grave, until a project led by Sir John's 'Magpie Group' (with the 'NUFC Fans United' supporters group in alliance) led to meetings with the club board, who agreed to help fund the cost of bringing the gates home. On 24th August 2013, prior to the opening home game of the season against West Ham, the gates were unveiled. Sir John and his Magpie Group, together with members of NUFC Fans United, were among those bearing witness to this great occasion. It was a big day, too, for Finlay McGhie, who was a special guest at the ceremony, courtesy of the Junior Magpies Young Supporters Club. Sir John said the gates "belonged to the fans" and Malcolm Dix from the Magpie Group stated that they would be a focal point for fans of all teams who visit St James' Park. In their new location outside the Milburn Stand, they were even blessed with Holy Water by Club Chaplain, Canon Glyn Evans—himself a huge fan of the club.

Wonga & NUFC staff with Malcolm Dix, Sir John Hall, Steve Hastie (NUFC Fans Utd) and mascot Finlay McGhie

'Magpie Group' John Waugh, Alan Rooney, Sir John Hall, Peter Ratcliffe and Malcolm Dix

Steve Wraith (NUFC Fans Utd)

Susan Snowdon, Ashley Joscelyne, Vicki Wilkin and Elaine Punton (NUFC Fans Utd)

Canon Glyn Evans - Blessing of the Gates

A kiss for Sir John from Angie

Chapter 13

A Love Affair in Black-and-White

The fans are the lifeblood of any club and Newcastle United fans are renowned as some of the most devoted in the country. Despite many years without any silverware or title trophies, and times when the faith has been truly tested, the fans have supported the team in their thousands. The club is the envy of most other Premiership teams who dearly wish they could count on such magnificent support through thick and thin. Here we meet a few dedicated followers for whom the players and the club form part of the very fabric of their everyday lives. A few stories and pictures to warm the cockles . . .

Rev James Errington

Jim is officially Newcastle United's oldest season ticket holder—having reached the grand age of 100 years in May 2015. Incredibly, he still travels to games by Metro train from his home in Kingston Park, Newcastle. He has been supporting the team for more than 85 years and has no plans to stop anytime soon. To celebrate his centenary, he was invited by Bobby Moncur for a special day in the Moncur Suite to watch the game against West Bromwich Albion on 9th May 2015. He loved every minute and showed incredible passion and energy, which left most of us feeling older than him! Jim first went to watch Newcastle in 1928 as a schoolboy. He recalls: "After that, I would go anytime I had a spare sixpence for the bus and sixpence to get into the ground". Jim, who was Church Minister at Denton Burn Methodist Church in Newcastle, bought his first season ticket in the 1980s, when they were first introduced. He has always loved the sheer passion and excitement on match days: "I've always loved going to the games. It's a marvellous atmosphere on match day—the buzz is just absolutely terrific. It's fascinating being there when the crowd is coming into stadium. If I had to choose my favourite ever player, I would say it has to be Hughie Gallagher, who played for the latter part of the 1920s. He was a marvellous player".

Jim enjoying 100th birthday celebration

Keith Talbot

"Why NUFC? Preston Hospital, North Shields is why. It's what we do, it's not negotiable. Once a Geordie, always a Geordie. My first visit to St James' Park was 1957. I have been through the lean years of Hollins, Alchurch,

White, Thomas et al (who was he?), sweetened by the Fairs Cup win with Wyn, Pop, Bobby. Little did we know that was to be the last of the big trophies! A move down South hasn't reduced my attendance. I go to every home game and around ten away games every season. The Keegan years provided respite from the barren times, but alas it brought nothing apart from the glory. Going to St James' isn't about cups or winning games, it's an obligation. I drive fifty miles to Kings Cross Station, London, then on to Newcastle Central Station and the stadium. I know many others who do similar journeys to follow their heroes. The privilege of watching Shearer—the greatest and most complete centre forward in world football—and Beardsley at his best, managed to offset the bad times. The magnet that is St James' Park is a powerful life-force. The attendance figures prove that immutable fact. Relative to lack of success, we are the best supported club in the world".

Keith at NUFC

Susan Snowdon

"My first memory of going to St James' Park was back in 1977, when I first put on a full NUFC strip and went to my first game with my school friend and her older brother. We went through the turnstile in the Gallowgate End armed with a scarf and a wooden rattle, which my dad had made for me especially for the day. It was painted black-and-white. The grass seemed so

Susan with treasured clock

green, the noise was deafening and the stadium was packed with fans. From that day to this, I still love the feeling when I walk up the stairs and see the grass and feel the same excitement when the players come out of the tunnel. It has now been thirty-eight years since my first game, and players and managers have come and gone, but the memories I have will never leave me. I remember going to Durham to watch the team training. I would go by myself and wait for my favourite player, Rob Lee, and each week I asked him for a photograph. One day, Terry McDermott came out and said to me, 'He's not here today'. My face sunk and, as I was walking away, he shouted 'Only joking!' I would go in all weathers and get photos taken with them all—and still do, to this day. I will never forget the day Ruud Gullit took Rob Lee's shirt number off him. I waited outside St James' Park and demanded that his shirt number be given back! I've made so many good friends over the years and shared many a debate over a pint in the Percy Arms trying to work out why we haven't won anything for years. On my trips around the country and Europe following the club, I was fortunate enough to get to know John Alder and last spoke to him on the way home from Wembley in 2014 after watching Gateshead play. Sadly, that was the last time I saw John alive before the horror MH17 disaster. At the auction of John's memorabilia, I sat patiently and was so happy when I purchased his prized Newcastle United clock, which came from his house. It is now hanging up in my house along with more than 200 photos of NUFC players, shirts and memorabilia. Of course, the best player for me was Rob Lee. Memories come and go with this club and I'm hoping that soon I will have a picture of us winning a trophy to display in my own hall of fame. I'm sure if I was cut open, my blood would be black-and-white. I love this club and always will".

Tony Scotland

"My earliest memories of going to St James' Park were as a 10-year-old around about 1970. I remember me and my mates getting to the ground about 11 o'clock when the place wasn't busy, so it was ideal for climbing over the fence at the Gallowgate End. We would hide in the toilets until the gates were open, then emerge onto the terraces. My earliest recollection of a game was a mid-week match against Doncaster Rovers in the 1973-4 season in the League Cup, as it was known back then. We won 6-0 with 'Supermac' Malcolm McDonald scoring a hat-trick. Best goal for me (and I can still see it after all these years) was a diving header by Ray 'Rocky' Hudson from outside the box at the Leazes End. I can't remember who it was against, but the goal is engraved in my memory. The game I look back on with sadness and sorrow—and the game that gave me most pleasure—were against the same team, Manchester United. The game in the 1995-6 season to me will always be the game that cost us the title that year, although I didn't realise it at the time. I remember the day like it was yesterday. The atmosphere was white-hot and there wasn't a single black-and-white fan in the ground that thought we would lose that day. We played them off the park. Should've been

Tony on his wedding day with Best Man Alec Irving

three-up at half-time, but we lost to a sucker punch 1-0, scored by Cantona at the back post. I feel sick just writing about it. However, the very next season, the 5-0 win against them was awesome, especially after the drubbing in the Charity Shield. I was in the Directors' Box that day and I have never seen champagne flow as it did. That game is still talked about with passion as if it was only played yesterday. Newcastle United is my true love. It is thought about every day, remembering the good, the bad and the downright ugly over the years, but it will always be there for me and I will always be there for it. No matter what. As I write this, it's just been confirmed that Steve McClaren is the new Head Coach. Let's all get behind him and look to what hopefully can be a great future—you've got to, haven't you?"

Tony even shared his Wedding Day with a very special guest—the Newcastle United Fire Engine!

Alan Cochrane

Alan is a member of Scottish-based supporters club 'Scottish Mags', which was set up around twelve years ago by Steven Carr for Newcastle United fans who lived north of the Border. Steven was keen to find 'Scottish Geordies' who wanted to travel to watch their team play either by train or car-sharing. The club has grown steadily over the years and Alan spoke to us of his dedication to following his beloved team: "I have been supporting Newcastle United since my very first game—I

Alan and Jackie Cochrane

remember it well—it was 9th December 1966. We played Chelsea in a 2-2 draw and I have been hooked ever since. At that time, I was eleven-years-old and lived in Spittal, near Berwick-upon-Tweed. My family moved to Edinburgh in 1971 but it didn't stop me from supporting the Toon. My favourite player, and the best I have seen at St James' Park, has to be Tony Green. His career was cut tragically short by injury far too young and he was an absolute genius on the ball. Over the years, I have travelled to as many games as possible, both to our home ground and others throughout the UK. I have also travelled to European games whenever possible. I met my wife Jackie in 1995 and she has been going to all the games with me ever since, as well. Sadly, she now suffers from multiple sclerosis, but that has not stopped her from joining me on trips to watch the team. She uses a wheelchair to go to games. We are both determined that nothing is going to stop us travelling to support our team".

Steven Carr and 'Scottish Mags' in Ukraine

Chapter 14

United in the Dales

Fans of the long-running ITV show Emmerdale will know that actors from the North East have figured prominently over recent years. We met up with four of the stars who are all dedicated followers of the black-and-whites. Long-serving actress Charlie Hardwick (Val Pollard), actor John Middleton (Rev Ashley Thomas), and more recent additions Laura Norton (Kerry Wyatt) and Bill Ward (James Barton), all attend St James' Park whenever they can.

Here are some of their memories of times at their own 'Theatre of Dreams':

Charlie Hardwick has had a season ticket in the Gallowgate End for many years. Charlie's mum, brother and sister took her to St James' Park in the 1970s, and she has remained a dedicated follower ever since. These days, she attends with her friends Kevin Miles, Chief Executive of the Football Supporters Federation, and Ged Grebby, who is involved with the 'Show Racism the Red Card' campaign. Some of her favourite players from over the years include John Tudor, Peter Beardsley, Les Ferdinand and Nobby Solano. Charlie has also travelled to away games in the UK and Europe over many seasons, and admits to being very vocal in her seat at the Gallowgate End. She has been known to start the singing on occasions and loves the social aspect of being a fan. Her passion for the club has never wavered—even during the difficult times. She also has great respect for the late and great Sir Bobby Robson: "He was a man of immense dignity, passion, cheek, and a little bit of stardust".

John Middleton has had a season ticket in the Gallowgate End since 2005. John has been a fan since 1967, when he moved to Newcastle with his family. He recalls: "In those days, they would open the gates fifteen minutes before the end of a match, so me and a mate used to sneak in". Now John attends games and regularly makes the round trip of some 160 miles from his home in Yorkshire on match days. His favourite players include Wyn Davies, Peter Beardsley and Alan Shearer. His favourite manager was Sir Bobby Robson, for obvious reasons. "But for sheer bonkers excitement, it has to be Kevin Keegan every time", John revealed with a smile. His favourite game is the now infamous 4-4 draw with Arsenal in 2011 when Newcastle came back from four goals down at half-time to draw the game. He recalls: "The first half was dismal and the second half heroic. Tiote's goal was stunning and Kevin Nolan came within inches of winning it. In the end, it felt like a fabulous win".

Laura Norton has been a fan from an early age, when her Dad Ron would take her to games. Laura is very proud of her Northern roots and believes the team is the lifeblood of the city, and that thousands of lives are affected each week by how well or how badly the team performs. She particularly loves watching games against the big clubs, such as Manchester United and Arsenal, when Newcastle United often produce a big surprise and win or draw games they were predicted to lose. She said: "I love it when they score a goal and the crowd rise up as one. It's a fabulous feeling and I want to experience that feeling as often as I possibly can". Laura would love the team to not just play in, but win a Wembley final, and she would love to be there to see it with her dad, Ron.

Bill Ward moved away from Newcastle when he started his acting career, but attends home games whenever he is on Tyneside to visit family and friends. When Bill was a young lad, he would be taken to games by his Dad. Sometimes they would be invited into the Directors Box with Gordon McKeag and at other times they'd go in the Leazes End—a big contrast for any fan. The camaraderie of the fans and the singing left a big impression on him. Over the years of attending games, he has sat in just about every part of the ground. His wider family of aunts, uncles and cousins are also fans, so he was following in the family tradition. He loves the magic of the FA Cup and it has been a big disappointment to him that the team have not fared so well in any of the domestic Cup competitions in recent years. His favourite time was the heady days of Kevin Keegan and his 'Entertainers'. He also loved the Bobby Robson years. Malcolm 'Supermac' Macdonald was the sort of exciting player that Bill loved to watch. He recalls seeing a banner at an FA Charity Shield game that read 'Mac 'll burst your nets'. Sadly, on that occasion, Supermac and Newcastle did not manage a victory, but the excitement of attending such a momentous occasion was something Bill will always treasure. Although he has not lived in his home city for many years, Bill does attend 'away' games whenever possible and has been to many stadiums in England when Newcastle United have been the visitors. He is very much looking forward to his next game at St James Park in 2015/16, and, as ever, is hoping this will be the year when the team will go on a decent FA Cup run. Maybe this time . . .

Hot off the Press!
Congratulations to Charlie, John, Laura and Bill and all cast and crew at 'Emmerdale'. Well done winning 'Best Soap' 2015.

Charlie Hardwick

John Middleton

Laura Norton

Bill Ward

Chapter 15

A Manager and a Fan—Jack Charlton, OBE

From a very early age Jack's mother, Cissie, introduced him to football. Almost as soon as he could walk, he would play football for hours in the streets of Ashington with his brother Bobby and his mother would often be seen playing with them. Jack's uncle first took him to a game at St James' Park as a young lad. Together, they would go to watch the team play, although the young Bobby often went to watch Sunderland. Jack always refused to go to Roker Park, though—until he had to play there. Jack was a very tall lad and developed his sometimes unorthodox defending skills as a teenager. He attracted the attention of several football scouts who were hardly ever away from Ashington to watch the young Charlton brothers hone their considerable talents. It was presumed that Jack would sign for Newcastle. However, his mother wanted him to go to Leeds because his uncles Jackie, George and Jim Milburn had all played for Leeds United, and she also knew it would be good for him to be away from home and be independent. After an illustrious playing career, having played a club record of 773 games for Leeds and won 35 caps for England and a World Cup winners medal, Jack's natural leadership skills ensured a smooth transition into football management with Middlesbrough FC. He led the team to the Second Division title in his first year of management. He was voted Manager of the Year in 1974.

Ten years later, in 1984, Jack came 'home' to Newcastle to manage the football team he had supported from childhood. Although his reign was all too brief, Jack recalls the feelings he had when he stood near the fans at home games: "Standing at the dugout on match days, you could feel the fans really close to you. You could even hear their banter, and you could see in their faces the excitement and the passion of being there, being part of the city and the club. Some folk who had heavy physical jobs all week—miners, foundry workers and suchlike—spent all week keeping going with the thoughts of being at the match at the weekend. They would shout for ninety minutes non-stop and, sometimes, they would let the players know exactly what they felt, if they weren't living up to expectations or made a lazy pass. Sometimes, the ones close to the dugout would tell you to make a substitution or change the tactics—and they were never afraid to let you know if they thought you weren't doing your job properly! I had plenty of banter with them. The Newcastle fans are very knowledgeable about their football and are, in my opinion, the most loyal and dedicated fans in the country. Many top teams have come to St James' Park and been totally overwhelmed by the noise and sheer

Jack and Bobby Charlton

passion of the home fans. Players from other clubs have told me they couldn't believe the noise when the teams came out of the tunnel, and so many have told me how they always looked forward to playing here. It was always such a big occasion and the fixture they always looked for at the start of the season. The atmosphere at St James' Park is second-to-none and better than any other ground I have known. The fans are a credit to the club and the city".

Jack still attends games as often as possible and we were delighted that he joined us in the Moncur Suite against Manchester United a couple of seasons ago, where he met up with legendary brother Bobby, who is a Director of Manchester United. Jack kept everyone at our table amused with his football stories, and fans young and old all wanted photos and autographs of the World Cup winner. To the Geordies, he will always be a popular hero and a hugely successful one, too.

Jack wearing his TOFFS scarf

Chapter 16

Across the Miles—Football Supporters' Federation

Kevin Miles has been a Newcastle fan ever since he can remember and has travelled thousands of miles over land and sea to watch his beloved Magpies. Having experienced the difficulties facing travelling fans, Kevin has worked tirelessly to ensure a better deal for fans throughout the country. He has a burning desire to provide a platform for fans and their rights, and has liaised with others to tackle important matters such as ticket pricing, safe standing and racism in football.

Kevin is currently Chief Executive of the Football Supporters Federation—known in football as the 'FSF'. The *Safe Standing Campaign, Twenty's Plenty for Away Tickets* and *Watching Football is not a Crime!* are splendid examples of issues with which the FSF is involved, helping fans across England and Wales, from top to bottom of the pyramid.

The organisation works in close collaboration with the likes of 'Kick It Out, 'Liberty' and 'Show Racism The Red Card', and is linked to fans internationally by their membership of 'Football Supporters Europe'. The FSF now has more than 500,000 members and you can join free of charge, or find out more, via their website at www.fsf.org.uk.

Kevin says:

"Fans of any club are the one constant that a club can boast. Players, managers, coaches, even owners and directors come and go, changing allegiance with each new contract or sale of shares. But supporters—with very rare and infamous exceptions—are with one club for life, for better or for worse. For me, that loyalty belongs to Newcastle United: that's my tribe, and I can't imagine a better one to be part of. There are precious few glory-hunters here, for obvious reasons. I've experienced my loyalty and commitment being exploited for the financial gain of others, but it has also given me so much joy over the years—with despair in at least equal measure—that it is a part of my being. Friendship, family, comradeship, all are bound up for me in this big black-and-white Geordie community".

Mark Prosser, Steve Grebby, Ged Grebby, Phil Jeffries and Kevin Miles – outside Steve's house in Finsbury Park before 1998 FA Cup Final

Chapter 17

The Foundation, Disabled Fans and Special Memories

The Foundation was founded in Summer 2008 when club owner Mike Ashley kick-started the funding with £50,000. It is an independent and registered charity, supported by Newcastle United Football Club. Its mission is to help disadvantaged children and families in the local area, by introducing them to sport and education and teaching how to live fit and healthy lives. Since it was formed, it has helped around 40,000 children develop a love of sport and it helps to support a number of growing initiatives: from wheelchair football to football coaching centres for the disabled. More recently, contributions from Northumbria Police and other organisations have helped sponsor the Cerebral Palsy and Downs Syndrome weekly football centres. It makes a huge difference to those it helps. One example is a young boy called Joe Reed. Joe suffers from cerebral palsy and he now plays football every week at the Walker Activity Dome with his new friends. He was chosen as a ball boy for the game against West Bromwich Albion the season of 2014/15. He told us: "The Foundation is really great and I feel privileged that such great schemes exist to help me play the game I love". His mum, Michelle, echoed his uplifting words: "The Foundation has enabled Joseph to realise he is not the only one with cerebral palsy and it has given him the confidence to make new friends and opportunities he would never have got before this". The children can also meet their favourite players, who regularly give time to the Foundation's many different projects. It has become a vital part of so many young lives through library-based learning initiatives and the 'Match Fit' programme aimed at improving the children's knowledge of the benefits of healthy food and exercise. Such opportunities would simply not exist without the Foundation. It can even prove a springboard for young sporting stars, as in the case of Jamie Foster whose potential has been spotted by the Great Britain Paralympics team. The Foundation is invaluable to the lives of those it helps by providing a sporting outlet. It helps build fitness, confidence and team work, as well as being a lot of fun for all involved.

Fans of the Foundation

The Newcastle United Disabled Supporters Association was set up in 1998 to help the club's disabled fans to follow and support the club they love. Over the years, it has grown from strength-to-strength. Through its work, the last fifteen years have seen vast improvements to the access and facilities at St James' Park to accommodate fans in wheelchairs and with other disabilities. These days, trips to away games are organised much better than previously and Newcastle's own disabled facilities compare very favourably with many other premier league grounds. Bringing people together is a very important aspect of the group. Four social events a year are organised,including the very special NUDSA Player of the Year award which is held at the end of each season at St James' Park. Last year's winner was Tim Krul, who followed in the footsteps of previous winners, including Alan Shearer and Fabricio Coloccini. Tim attended the function and spent time with the fans, many of whom wore orange to make Dutchman Krul feel right at home. Tim thoroughly enjoyed the evening, as did the fans, and it was a magical night with the goalkeeper posing for photographs and answering questions from the fans. Stephen Miller, paralympian and dedicated United follower, is the Club Secretary and is very active along with his mum, Rosalynd, and the rest of the committee, who deal with disabled issues across the board.

Joe Reed and Jackie Milburn Statue

James Marshall is a young man who lost an eye to cancer, but he has always been enthusiastic and determined to live a very full life. He spent an unforgettable day as a club mascot for the game against Swansea in May 2015. His proud mum, Julie, took him to St James' Park for his special day and said: "James absolutely loved his day as a mascot for his favourite team, Newcastle United. He enjoyed meeting all of his favourite players, especially

Moussa Sissoko and Jack Colback. It was a dream-come-true for him and he was so overwhelmed about the whole day from start to finish. The best part for James was walking out onto the pitch with Sissoko holding his hand and then having a kick-about with him. He never stopped smiling the whole time and we all have great memories for the rest of our lives. Thanks to the West Wylam Football Club, aka 'Tip Top', for the memorable week that we will never forget".

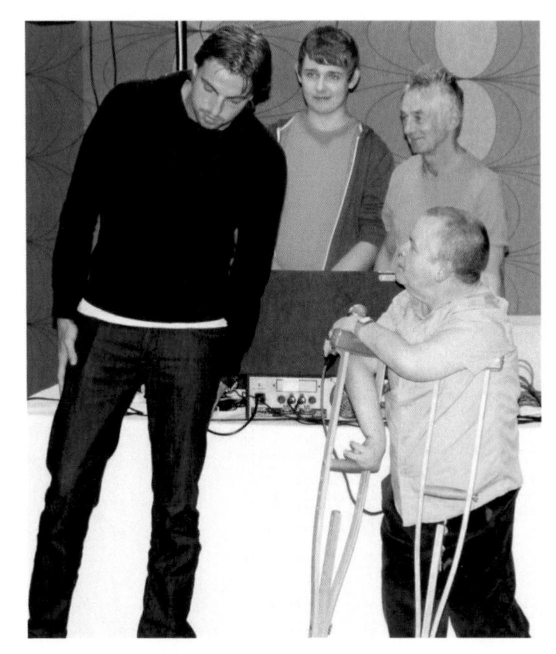

Tim Krul and Gareth Beard

James Marshall, Mascot

Harry Luckhurst with Hatem Ben Arfa

Harry Luckhurst is totally blind and, although he was not born in Newcastle, he decided that he wanted to follow the Magpies from an early age. Harry goes to as many games as possible and explains just what being a fan means to him: "My name is Harry Luckhurst and I'm twenty-six-years-old. Despite living in the South East of England, I have followed Newcastle United since I was young. I am completely blind and, for that reason, I used to go to games with family or friends from the South. The first time I went to a game on my own was actually the first time I had travelled long distance without a sighted guide. It really opened my eyes (excuse the pun) to what a person can achieve, despite a disability. I have met some great friends who I still know very well to this day. Despite having a very close family and set of friends, I have never felt anything like the camaraderie that you feel at a game, whether it's in the pub beforehand or at the match itself. Football is such a great tool for bringing people together, and a great ice-breaker to meet people. Sometimes, I wish that I had chosen a team a little closer to home, so I could get the experience of going to a home game regularly and truly hating your rivals. Although I'm sure if I have to sit through any more 'derby games' like the last few, this won't be a problem! I would never change my club, though, especially now I have it tattooed on me".

Chapter 18

More Magic Football Memories

The dictionary definition of a 'football supporter' is "a person who is actively interested in, and wishes success for, a particular football team"—a description that is more than appropriate for many of the fans who have contributed to this book.

Charles Davis is one such fan and he has supported the club since he was a young lad. For the last 26 years, he has watched games from his executive box, and was one of the very first fans to use the corporate facilities. In fact, on the first occasion the boxes were available for use, Charles remembers Club Director, Gordon McKeag, calling in to check that everything was in order and working satisfactorily. Charles mentioned that there did not appear to be a supply of electricity, to which McKeag replied: "Never mind, as long as the players are switched on—that's what matters". Apart from this, and a few other mi-

Charles Davis 70th birthday with framed shirt presented by Kevin Keegan

nor teething problems, Charles has enjoyed entertaining friends, family and business colleagues over the years, and welcoming some of Angie's guests, following their afternoon in the Moncur Suite. His greatest memory was being invited onto the pitch on his 70th birthday, and given a signed shirt, with his age and surname on the back. It was presented by Kevin Keegan and was a very proud moment for Charles and his family. On the way to the pitch, Charles remembers meeting the future England Manager, Roy Hodgson, in the players' tunnel. Roy wished him a happy birthday and Charles was delighted. Over the years, he has experienced the highs and lows at St James' Park. Len White, Peter Beardsley and Paul Gascoigne stand out as some of his favourite players.

David Waugh is another fan who has supported the club for many years. He often takes along his young grandson, Ben, thus following in the family tradition since David's father took him to games at a young age. David recalls: "My father began taking me to home games in 1946/47—the first season after the war, when we were then in the old Division 2. I remember the 13-0 win against Newport County with Len Shackleton scoring six, including a hat-trick in three minutes. True to form, we lost the return game and failed to get promotion until the next season. In those days, we had to get to the ground two hours before kick-off, so I could sit on the front wall that surrounded a 'ditch' that separated the crowd from the pitch (pre-health and safety days!). Later, in a crowd of over 67,000, versus Liverpool, I was passed over everyone's heads down to the front. And, on another occasion, I lost a tooth and was passed the other way. I recall several seasons standing in the Leazes End

David Waugh and grandson Ben

'shed' and then many more being caught in crowd surges in the Gallowgate End. I now appreciate the comfort of the Moncur Suite! My best memories have to be being at Wembley to see us lift the FA Cup three times in five years in the early 1950s and, especially, those two 'Wor Jackie' goals against Blackpool. Sixty years later, and I still live in hope!"

Paul Martin is a Geordie singer/songwriter who now lives in Majorca. He has supported Newcastle since boyhood and watches games on TV whenever possible. He attends games on his regular trips home to Newcastle when visiting his family. Paul has written songs for both Sir Bobby Robson and Alan Shearer and he performed some of his own songs at the opening night of 'Shearer's Bar' in 2004. He also recorded a song for the cup final in 1999. He met Sir Bobby several times and was delighted that Bobby told him how much he enjoyed the songs he had written for him. Paul's dream is to sing his Newcastle songs on the St James' Park pitch in the white-hot atmosphere before a 'derby' game against Sunderland. He said it would be a "dream come true" for him to entertain the Geordie faithful, before such an important game.

Paul Martin and Sir Bobby Robson

Dale Meeks is an actor/musician who has supported Newcastle since he was a lad. Dale said: "The first football match I ever attended was in 1991, around the age of 16. My parents were both devotees of musical theatre. So, in the Meeks household, we were more inclined to hear 'Some Enchanted Evening' rather than 'Howay the Lads'. As a child, I lived in Cleadon, which has a Sunderland postcode. I remember being dressed in Sunderland hat and scarf in the winter—although, given time and a cracking physiotherapist, I've managed to erase those memories! Best game ever was when I was in Manchester filming a movie, and our work was due to finish on the Saturday evening—leaving plenty of time to get home for the big game at St James' Park against Man United the following day. However, due to a fire on set, we were unable to complete the film, and had to watch the game in our Manchester hotel, as we had to stay an extra week. The atmosphere in the hotel bar that afternoon, deep within the enemy territory of Manchester, was electric. A bunch of young Geordie actors cheered their hearts out as their team won 5-0, with hotel staff looking on in obvious dismay at their team's humiliation. It was one of the best moments of my life.

Dale Meeks

My favourite player of all time has to be Paul Gascoigne, simply for THAT goal against Scotland during Euro 1996. I was there in person and have to say I've never seen a better moment in football, before or since. I also had the pleasure of meeting Sir Bobby Robson one time and he was charming and kind with a magnetic personality. He is dearly missed, but his legacy lives on. What a wonderful man!"

'Run Geordie Run' - Mark Allison is a fan who has become widely known for running great distances to raise hundreds of thousands of pounds for the Sir Bobby Robson Foundation and Children's charities. He ran across Australia and then America, where he famously covered 3,100 miles in 100 days. Newcastle United fans, based in New York, ran the final 13 miles with Mark on the last day of the run. He is currently in training to embark on another similar fundraising effort in 2016. He told us: "My fascination/obsession/sense of duty/love for Newcastle United started in the mid-1980s when Willie McFaul was the manager. I remember idolising Peter Beardsley at the time and was devastated, as a fifteen-year-old, when he left for Liverpool. Following the team has been much like my 20,000 miles charity run around the world: a series of incredible highs matched almost entirely with crushing lows. All the while, though, an immense feeling of local pride has been evident. Despite the lack of silverware, I wouldn't swap supporting my home town team with any of the more successful teams in the country".

Mark Allison and NUFC fans from New York almost 'over the line'

Den Jolly is another dedicated fan who hails from North Shields and emigrated to Sydney, Australia with wife Lesley in the early 1980s. This distance from the town of his birth has only served to increase his passion for his beloved team. The advent of the internet in the mid-1990s was a Godsend for him and thousands of other expats, keen to keep bang up-to-date with the exploits on the pitch. Den now watches live games at all hours of the Australian night and early morning in his specially adapted 'Newcastle United Cave', which is a room dedicated to all things black-and-white and with a suitably widescreen TV. Unfortunately, his attempts to see Newcastle United win at St James' Park on trips back home have been fairly unsuccessful, leading to what family members now refer to as 'The Jolly Jinx'. Take the 2013/14 season, for example. Den flew from Australia to England and went direct from Newcastle airport to watch his team play Hull City, only to witness a painful 3-2 defeat. When he returned to England the following February, he was again just in time to see Newcastle hammered 3-0 and stayed on Tyneside long enough to watch the 4-0 thrashing by Spurs. Typically, and perhaps luckily for the team, Den flew home on the afternoon of the home game against Aston Villa. He had just left British airspace when Loic Remy scored a late winner to give the Magpies all three points. Unlucky Den has not seen his team win live in over 20 different trips back to England. His best result was a point against Birmingham at an away game in 2008. Let's hope he doesn't get a ticket if we get to Wembley anytime soon!

Den Jolly, 3rd right, with family at NUFC

Den has asked us to give a special mention to the website www.nufc.com, which provides a brilliant service for fans around the world like Den, as well as for local fans. Biffa and Niall, 'your genial hosts', were too modest to be interviewed, yet provide an invaluable platform of information and their web-

John Tudor, wife Anne and Mick Hill of the Strawberry Pub

site is often the first port of call for many a Newcastle fanatic both home and abroad. We are delighted to include them here and congratulate them on behalf of all the fans for their daily dedication to keeping us informed with breaking news from St James' Park. Another place worth mentioning here is the famous watering hole, 'The Strawberry', which is bedecked in Newcastle United memorabilia and is right next to St James' Park. 'Mine Host' Mick and his staff provide a fantastic football-themed atmosphere, and the roof terrace gives a perfect view of the stadium. Fans from all over the country and abroad head for the pub on match-days and the place teems with black and white shirts, everywhere you look. The atmosphere is truly black-and-white and you can have a few pints and great food prior to the game. Many of the players have frequented the pub over the years, and now there will be even more space soon as an upstairs function room has just been opened, which has its own bar and is perfect for a big celebration. Earlier this year I went to the pub with that great player from the '70s, John Tudor, and his wife Anne. They were on a visit from America, where they have lived for many years. They received the warmest of welcomes and chatted for a good while with the owner, Mick Hill, who (you will not be surprised to know) is also a massive fan of the club.

Steve Hunter is an exiled Geordie living in America. He has lived in Dallas for eleven years since moving from Newcastle in 2004 and is an art teacher. He told us: "I moved to Dallas in 2004, leaving behind my beloved Newcastle United. Not for long, though—I used to watch the games on TV whenever possible and, during 2010, I made friends with some other guys who were fans. I set up a Facebook site called 'Toon Army Dallas' to find more expat fans. We regularly meet in 'The Dubliner' pub in Lower Greenville, Dallas, to watch the games and cheer the lads back home. Around forty of us meet for games. I was then asked to set up a 'Toon Army America' page, which is now the main site, and I was delighted to do so. There are now more than 3,000 followers on the sites, while more sites are being added from many parts of America. It was a big highlight to watch the games on Newcastle United's pre-season trip to the States in Summer 2015. I am delighted to provide some photos for this book of the fans meeting the players at various places on their tour. I love the club as much as ever and always will".

Toon Army Dallas

Toon Army Chicago

Toon Army Philadelphia

Chapter 19

Chapter and Verse in Black and White

Fans are many and varied. There are some whose thoughts are never far away from their team, even when penning their next best-sellers! Two of our region's top crime writers borrow the surnames of former Newcastle players for fictional characters in their books. Howard Linskey and Mari Hannah have supported the Magpies for as long as they can remember. They have put pen to paper and told us, in their own words, what they feel about their club.

Howard Linskey - "I blame my Uncle Neil. He got me into Newcastle United and then brought me back a programme from the 1974 FA Cup Final. We lost, but it didn't matter. I was hooked early and have been ever since. I will never forget walking up the steps of St James' Park and seeing that hallowed turf below me for the first time. I've still not experienced anything that compares with the raw emotion of standing amongst thousands of fellow Toon fans and roaring on the black-and-whites together. I've seen Newcastle surrender a twelve-point lead in the Premiership, attended two FA Cup Finals, two semi-finals, plus a Charity Shield—and we lost the lot. I have borne the pain of relegation three times and endured countless away trips to football's less glamorous destinations. Then came the 'glory years' under Kevin Keegan and, later, Bobby Robson. My personal all-time highs include the 5-0 thrashing of Manchester United, thumping Sunderland 5-1 and watching Keith Gillespie helping Tino Asprilla to destroy Barcelona. My personal heroes include Supermac, Kevin Keegan, Peter Beardsley, Rob Lee, Les Ferdinand and Shay Given and, arguably the very best of them all, Alan Shearer. I became a 'published' writer in *The Mag* fanzine way back in 1989. Now I'm an author with Penguin who names his characters after obscure Newcastle United players, to the bemusement of my publisher. Shame I can't write us a proper happy ending with a trophy-winning season. Maybe it will happen one day. I only hope I won't be too old to enjoy it".

Howard Linskey

Mari Hannah - "My earliest memory of Newcastle United was the Inter-Cities Fairs Cup game against Ujpest Dozsa back in the glory days. It was the beginning of my love affair with the club. My two sons are avid supporters. I bought their first season tickets, ensuring my status as the best mum in the world. Despite disappointing results and no silverware in recent years, our passion for the club hasn't diminished. Real Newcastle fans will turn up regardless, as they did in the nail-biting final game of the 2014-15 season. I was there when

Mari Hannah

they beat West Ham. It felt very special to share the ecstasy of that moment with the best fans in the world. There's nothing like the roar of a capacity crowd—except, perhaps, a great escape from relegation. Who wouldn't want to be part of that? I'm reaching for the tissues just thinking about it".

Paul Joannou is the official Club Historian for Newcastle United and, over the years, he has written books for the fans sharing his vast knowledge of facts, figures and information about the club and its players. Paul is also very much a fan, too. He told us; "Born a Geordie, always a Geordie, even in exile. Proud to have black-and-white blood and support my home town club. It's a Tyneside institution in our corner of England, with such a rich tradition and colourful story since 1881. And all despite the never-ending and intense frustration at watching the Magpie soap-opera . . . when will they ever get it right!?"

Paul Joannou

Anne Graham is another local writer and Magpies fan. Her book, *My North East By Its Famous Sons And Daughters* was published in 2013, in aid of the 'Sir Bobby Robson Foundation'. It was Waterstone's number one best-seller in North-East England in December that year. Anne told us: "I may get drummed out of the Brownies for saying this (actually, I was drummed out of the Brownies at school so it wouldn't be the first time), but our season in the Championship in 2009-10 was one of my favourites. Of course, it started horribly. The disgrace of relegation followed by the death of Sir Bobby Robson formed a gloomy backdrop to the coming season, coupled with widespread worries of a Leeds-style plummet down the tables. But, instead, we gathered a seemingly unstoppable head of steam and cruised joyfully towards a top finish. Away games became something to look forward to, with carnival atmospheres in the pubs pre-match, grounds with old-school terracing, lots of singing and happy journeys home. The fans' solidarity was matched by team-spirit on the pitch, and we had real heroes to salute like Kevin Nolan and our dignified manager, Chris Hughton. As the crowds belted out 'We Are The Champions' on the final day of the season, I wondered whether we'd get a chance to sing it again, at the top level or in a cup. I pray we do. It's our club after all—no matter whose name is on the title deeds".

Anne Graham

Chapter 20

The Love of a Lifetime—John Alder and Liam Sweeney

The first anniversary of the Malaysia Airlines MH17 disaster, in which 298 souls lost their lives when an aircraft was shot down in July 2014 over Ukrainian airspace, occurred during the writing of this chapter. One year on, the families of John Alder and Liam Sweeney have experienced significant life changes, some of which they could not imagine would ever happen to them. The families have dealt not only with the grief of losing their loved ones, but also found solace and comfort alongside other families who suffered, too, on that fateful day. During the last year, Liam's dad, Barry, has travelled to meet with parents of other victims and attend memorial services, both at home and abroad. The outpouring of grief shown by fellow fans around the world, and the bonding of Newcastle United and Sunderland fans, united in respect for John and Liam, has proved that, beyond all doubt, whatever team we support, we share respect for other fans, regardless of local or national rivalries.

Sunderland fans certainly played their part with a great gesture organised by Black Cats fan, Gary Ferguson. He set up a crowd-funding scheme, initially in order to raise £100 for a floral tribute—but managed to raise a staggering amount in excess of £33,000, which he donated equally between the Sir Bobby Robson Foundation and Marie Curie Cancer Care. Many Sunderland fans also brought shirts and flowers to St James' Park. Fan opposition was forgotten and grief shared for these special circumstances.

Tributes to John and Liam at St James' Park

John and Liam were a familiar sight to other fans, especially to Newcastle's ardent 'away' following. John had an incredible record of attending games. Since 1974, he missed only one match home or away. That was when he had to divert his plans in order to be with his mum, when her health had taken a turn for the worse. Liam demonstrated similar levels of devotion with his active involvement as a steward on supporters' buses to away games. The club acted very quickly to recognise the total commitment of these two fans; A memorial site sprang up outside the Milburn Stand. Fans in their hundreds brought floral tributes and football scarves. This was followed by manager, Alan Pardew, and captain, Fabricio Coloccini, laying a wreath at the seats Liam and John would have occupied at their destination in the stadium in Wellington, New Zealand. On their return, the United manager and captain were joined by other club officials at the funeral service. Newcastle United continued the club's tribute with a minute's silence before the first home game of the season against Man City, during which the close family of both men joined the players on the pitch. The supporters showed their respects when a fan-organised 17th minute applause became a feature at both home and away games throughout the season. The new screen in the stadium also displayed shirts with the names of both men at regular intervals during games. The Alder/Sweeney Memorial Garden was officially opened by Newcastle United in 2014, to ensure that they will always be etched into club folklore.

Alder and Sweeney Families on the pitch for NUFC tribute

John was an avid collector of Newcastle United merchandise and his family decided to auction the memorabilia for charity. Hundreds of fans attended the event in the Moncur Suite and the incredible amount of £26,000 was raised. John's sister, Joyce Robbins, bought her brother's scarf as a personal keepsake. Afterwards, she said: "This collection, and following Newcastle United, meant the world to John and we wanted to do something special with it. The whole family agreed it should be donated to charity. We hope the people who buy the different lots treasure this memorabilia, as John did. We're very proud that John's enthusiasm will go on to help other people through the Sir Bobby Robson Foundation". The auction was a marvellous gesture and another flower of hope to emerge from the tragedy.

To mark the first anniversary, Geordie singer Junior Turner recorded a song in tribute to the lads. 'United We Stand' is available on CD from the 'Back Page' shop and also via iTunes. Funds raised will benefit several charities.

Barry's wife Lesley, has written a moving tribute to Liam and John and she gave her blessing for these heartfelt words to be included in this book:

Liam is Dead But Not Gone

He took to the skies
With his Geordie Mate John
To watch their beloved Toon
In a pre-season friendly

Liam is dead but not gone

They were travelling to faraway lands
Not knowing the skies they were in
Were full of hate and war-torn areas

Liam is dead but not gone

They were excited and happy
A trip of a lifetime
Probably even a bit tipsy—I hope

Liam is dead but not gone

A bang and a crash
Then no more light
Just debris and carnage
They were dead but not gone

Liam is dead but not gone

His soul is still there watching
The games at St James' Park
Back to his beloved Toon
His black-and-white world
Back where he belongs

Barry Sweeney – 17th Minute Applause for John and Liam

Strawberry Pub Tribute Board for John and Liam

'United' Black/white and Red/white Floral Tribute

Chapter 21

Sir Bobby Robson—The Fans Tribute

"What is a club in any case? Not the buildings or the directors or the people who are paid to represent it. It's not the television contracts, get-out clauses, marketing departments or executive boxes. It's the noise, the passion, the feeling of belonging, the pride in your city. It's a small boy clambering up stadium steps for the very first time, gripping his father's hand, gawping at that hallowed stretch of turf beneath him and, without being able to do a thing about it, falling in love"

Sir Bobby Robson, CBE

In July 2009, Newcastle-upon-Tyne lost one of its favourite sons and father figures when Sir Bobby Robson lost his long fight against cancer. Newcastle United opened the gates of St James' Park to mourning fans, initially for one weekend. But for several days, there was a glorious, multi-coloured football-shirt tribute from all corners of the world. Strips from Barcelona, Lisbon, Eindhoven, Fulham and Ipswich were swathed among the seating, and a whole host of Newcastle and England shirts, banners and scarves bedecked part of the stadium. Despite having to queue for several hours, almost 50,000 well-wishers visited the shrine over that weekend, and club bosses decided to keep the ground open until the following Thursday to allow even more people to pay their respects. Lady Elsie Robson and her sons came to witness the outpouring of respect for a man who was universally loved by fans, players and fellow managers alike. A giant shirt draped over many rows of seats was signed by hundreds of fans with heartfelt messages of love and condolence.

Giant Shirt – Tribute to a Giant of a Man

Sir Bobby was a player whose leadership qualities led to a seamless switch to management. He took charge of such great clubs as Barcelona and PSV Eindhoven, following his hugely successful spell as manager of Ipswich Town, and he even guided Newcastle United to Champions League qualification. He both played for and managed England. With three Geordies in the team (Peter Beardsley, Chris Waddle and Paul Gascoigne), his team only narrowly lost on penalties to West Germany, in that epic semi-final in Italia '90. He came closer than any other manager since 1966 to winning the World Cup again for England. He was awarded a CBE and Knighthood for services to football from the Queen, and inducted as a member of the English Football Hall of Fame in 2003. In 2005, he was made an Honorary Freeman of the city of Newcastle-upon-Tyne. The citation was as follows: "In recognition of his long and outstanding career across Europe, his role as an ambassador for the North East and Newcastle, and his contribution to the culture and life of the city". In 2007, he was awarded the BBC Sports Personality of the year Lifetime Achievement Award and, in 2008, was honoured as Freeman of the Borough of Ipswich and Freeman of the city of Durham.

The Fans Pay Homage to Sir Bobby

Most of all, Bobby was a man of great humanity, who had time for everyone he met. Typically, when he was suffering from cancer, he set up the Sir Bobby Robson Foundation, a cancer research charity, which has collected more than seven million pounds for the cause. It is still raising funds in his memory to carry on the work he started.

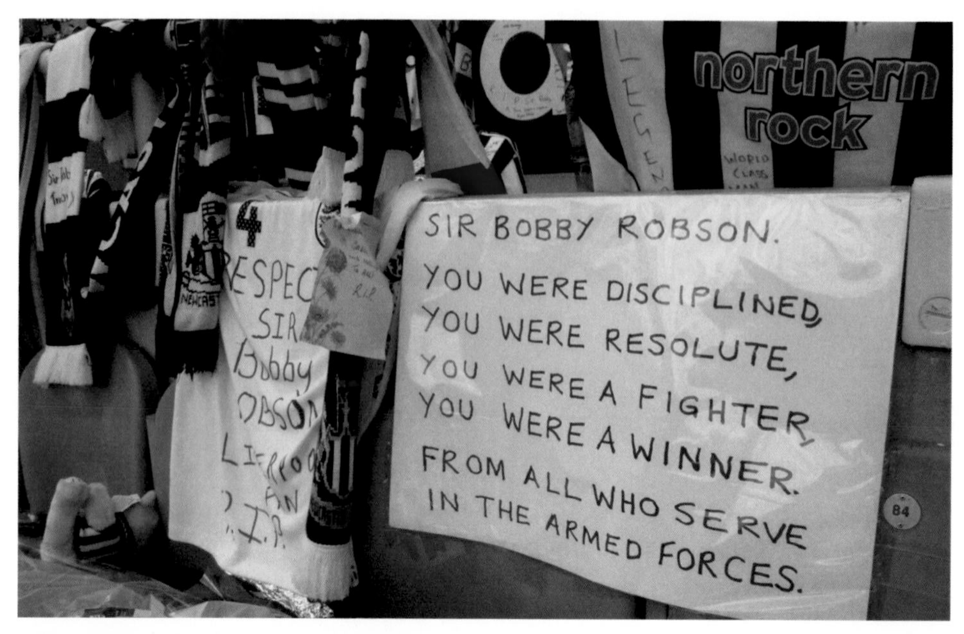

Tribute to Sir Bobby from HM Armed Forces

Sir Bobby with son Mark at Vila Sol, Portugal, 2009

Sir Bobby with sons Andrew and Paul at Tynemouth, Tyne and Wear

Newcastle United's legendary striker, Alan Shearer, had great admiration and respect for Sir Bobby. When asked if he would give us some words to sum up the great man, he told us:

"The whole world loves Sir Bobby, not just football. He radiated that sort of warmth. A man with a twinkle in his eye and a word for everyone. His great strength was man management. He was a master at that. Whether it be a senior pro or a young lad, Bobby knew how to get the best out of him. He had time for you and made you feel good. I remember, after he took over as manager of Newcastle United, he sat me down in my London hotel room. We were playing Chelsea and he spoke passionately about what he wanted and how he would go about getting it. He did the same with most of the others. Did it work? Well, on his first game at home before Newcastle fans, we won 8-0 and I scored five! I guess it did.

A lot is made of Bobby mixing up people's names but I'm not certain it wasn't an act. He was a clever man who liked to get a reaction. When he was diagnosed with cancer, Bobby set up his Foundation as his way of confronting it. He was always a fighter.

His death brought a public outpouring of grief and, a little while later, when I was approached by the Robson family to take over as the Foundation's patron, I was honoured. To follow in the footsteps of such a great man is simply a privilege".

Alan Shearer
Sir Bobby Robson Foundation Patron

Sir Bobby and Lady Elsie at a fundraising Ball in 2005

Chapter 22

A Blessing in Disguise!

Every club has a Chaplain who gives support and guidance to players of all creeds and religions. At Newcastle United they have someone who is not only a man of the cloth, but also a dedicated supporter who is not shy to celebrate that fact in his everyday life and work. He was invited by Sir John Hall to 'bless the gates' when they were re-erected at the stadium in 2013. This is an extract from his own personal gospels.

"My name is Reverend Canon Glyn Evans and I am a passionate Newcastle United fan. I believe that even Jesus was a football fan. Jesus had twelve disciples and got rid of Judas so he had a team of eleven—known locally as Bethlehem FC! Often, people talk about the hallowed turf and football being a religion. I can see many comparisons with religion and football. There is the passion, the agony and, of course, keeping the faith. Like most football fans, I live in hope of one day winning the league or cup! My passion for Newcastle led me to write hymns about Newcastle United. I changed the words from traditional hymns to ones appropriate for the club. I was bestowed with the honour of 'Barclaycard Fan of the Month' for these hymns.

We are passionate as a family about the club and so we named our son Ossie after the great Ossie Ardiles, whom we loved as our manager. We nearly named our daughter Keegan. Over the years, there have been many passionate moments as a fan. Our trips to Wembley were highlights in the 90's, but we saw only one goal from Robert Lee—but it felt like going to heaven! Of course, there have been great players and not so great. Three players for whom I always have a soft spot are, firstly, Mirandinha, the first Brazilian footballer to play here; secondly, Micky Quinn, a real character and goalscorer; and, thirdly, my favourite player, David Kelly, who scored a hat-trick against Leicester City (his former club) on the last day of our 1993 league-winning season under Kevin Keegan. He has been my favourite player because of his hard work and passion.

'Bless Our Club' – Canon Glyn Evans with Holy Water

The passionate days under Kevin Keegan were, of course, a highlight, but there are many days of excitement and despair I have shared with family and friends in the years spent following Newcastle United. I look forward to many more passionate days and heavenly moments".

Chapter 23

50 Shades of Black and White

by Stuart Latimer

It's in my blood, Newcastle United, and my love affair with the club began before I could run or kick a ball, watching old videos with my Dad of the 1983/4 promotion season, featuring the holy trinity of Kevin Keegan, Peter Beardsley and Chris Waddle. Wearing my first strip, learning to play the game in the back garden and viewing highlights from subsequent seasons from Gazza's Genius to Mirandinha Magic was all part of my magical apprenticeship in supporting Newcastle. The only problem was my Dad only taped the highlights when Newcastle won, so I was about 8 or 9 before I knew Newcastle *could* even lose. A shock to the system, yet normal service was resumed when Keegan took over as Manager.

Luton Town at home was my first game as a late substitute for my brother, Chris, and I took pride of place sitting on the bollards at The Gallowgate End to watch Kenny Wharton score the winner, hugging my Dad when we won.

One of my favourite ever Newcastle United moments involves two great men, my father and Alan Shearer. It wasn't at the match, though, but when the phone rang at home in the summer of 1996. It was my Dad excitedly telling me to check Teletext. Switching the old BBC Ceefax onto page 302, the blue flashing headline read 'Shearer Signs for Newcastle for World Record £15M'. The rest is history. Alan Shearer remains my joint favourite ever Newcastle player tied with Peter Beardsley and the 5-0 win against Manchester United my favourite match, with unsung hero Shola Ameobi worthy of a special mention, and the Sunderland 5-1 demolition derby a close second. My Dad's footballing hero has always been Malcolm Macdonald so it was a nice surprise when SuperMac himself married into the family, strengthening the NUFC connections.

Maureen Latimer and Nobby Solano

Truly, there have been some tough times following Newcastle and there's nothing worse than trudging home in the rain or snow when we've lost to a last-minute goal or, worse, a refereeing howler. Regular readers of my articles and blogs on the web will know my thoughts on Newcastle not getting our fair share of key decisions and penalties. Normally my Dad doesn't attend friendlies or testimonials, only competitive matches, so I was brought up with the mentality that the football results, recorded in

Stuart and Shola Ameobi

his own book of stats and tables, matters. It's where Shankly got the idea from, I believe . . .

Essentially testing my commitment to the Newcastle cause, my Dad always parked as far as is humanly possible away from St James' Park on match days. Then we'd walk in over the Town Moor and through Exhibition Park, with talk about the teams building anticipation and atmosphere on the way to the pub or stadium. It is always worth it when you enter the ground and hear the first strains of 'Local Hero' as the players come out – especially under the floodlights of a night game, which are always better. That moment is un-

Stuart with his 'local hero' Alan Shearer

matchable when the ball hits the back of the net and you celebrate in primal unison with 50,000 Geordie souls and bask in that top-of-the-world feeling when we win.

Chris, Ian and Stuart Latimer

I'd like to take this opportunity to thank my Dad, Ian, for passing on to me his own amazing passion for Newcastle United, taking me to all the games and putting up with sitting next to me all these years. My brother, Chris, sits with us now and I'm sure his new baby son Jack will continue the family tradition – he'll have no choice! I'm Mr Positivity at the match and Chris is Mr Negativity, while my Dad is pretty level-headed and realistic, having seen it all over the last 50 years. My optimism remains that he will see us win the League and Cups one day soon and have all his dedication rewarded.

Baby Jack in his natural 'Shearer Salute' pose

I'd also like to thank our genial host and author, Angie, who has changed my Magpies-supporting life and world in general since she scouted me for the Celebrity Football Passion 'Dream Team' a few years ago. We've shared lots of magical football moments with Bob Moncur, Lady Elsie Robson and her sons, and a galaxy of stars at St

James' Park. It certainly has had its perks - seeing Jade Thirlwall at our table after another defeat to Sunderland really helped soften the blow ... God knows I needed cheering up then! So I'd like to extend thanks to Angie from everyone in this book whom she's featured, hosted at matches and helped in many football-related ways through her love, generosity and charitable contributions.

I remain an ultra-optimistic fan and I'm 100% sure the best is yet to come on the Toon Rollercoaster, for everyone connected with the mighty Newcastle United.

Don't Stop Believin'...

email me : GeordieLegend@hotmail.com
and follow me on Twitter : @ultrastartime

Stuart Latimer

Stuart and Angie celebrate the win over West Ham, 2015

Chapter 24

A Labour of Love and Thanks …

It has taken four years to finally complete this 'labour of love'. It began when I decided to marry my love for football and writing in order to pay homage to every one of the devoted fans who love Newcastle United. Being a fan has brought me such joy, excitement and passion. I have felt part of a huge, dedicated family whose very fabric of life is intertwined with the club. The joy, the pain and the sheer outpouring of emotion at every game brings a precious and life-enhancing quality to being part of the football community that is unmatchable. It has been a wonderful journey so far, and one I hope will last forever.

How to thank special friends and family, who have inspired, encouraged and believed in me? I will try my very best to do so in this chapter. But whatever words I use, they will never be enough to demonstrate my thanks and gratitude. The first person to be mentioned here has to be my dear departed dad, Les. He took me to my first game in 1969, when I was a young schoolgirl. The experience will stay etched in my memory forever. It was an evening game and we were playing Vitoria Setubal of Portugal in the European Fairs Cup. We set off on the bus and it was snowing heavily. My mum was worried I would catch cold and miss school the next day. Dad found us a great vantage- point near the back of the Leazes End and we arrived just in time to see the players run onto the pitch. It was so exciting. The power-

Angie's Dad, Les, who introduced her to football

ful floodlights in the snow-filled skies were magical: I was awe-struck by the fact that each player had four shadows. As soon as we scored, I felt a rush behind us. I was swept forward and held on tight to my dad. The crowd attendance that night was more than 57,000—it was so exciting and the happiness on the faces of the hard-working Geordies was a joy to behold. We won 5-1 and my lifetime love affair had begun. From then on, the football die was cast for me. I prayed dad would take me to more games—but he worked on a Saturday, so it was evening games only, which were few and far between. A few years later, my mum wrote to the club to see if they had jobs on a Saturday for young people that included watching the game! She did brilliantly and found my dream Saturday job as a 'Golden Girl'. My friend Rosemary and I had to follow 'Don, the peanut man' around the pitch and sell golden-goal tickets. We were allowed to watch the game from the player's tunnel. Imagine that! You could hear just about everything the manager said to the players. No way in today's security-conscious world would that be possible ... So a big thank-you, dad—you introduced me to all this and I dedicate this to you. I know you are watching over me.

My love of writing was fashioned not just by my mum Aileen, but by someone who can make words dance on a page before you, and create the thrills and the passion of the written word like no-one else I know. John Gibson, who has dedicated his working life to reporting on his favourite team, Newcastle United, for the Newcastle Chronicle has been not just a friend, but a massive inspiration. Thank you, John, for your constant encouragement and belief in me. The thanks are much overdue, but no less heartfelt.

Angie at The Chronicle's 'Player of the Month' Lunch with Chris Waddle and Joe Harvey

A special mention must be made here to someone who has helped me to create this book. I met Stuart Latimer a few years ago, and his talent for writing was evident from the start. His sheer enthusiasm and gift for expression have kept me going at certain times when the going was tough. Luckily, the tough didn't get going and Stuart's contribution has been just what I needed to get this book 'over the line'. Thanks for your considerable efforts, Stuart, to bring this to print—you must take a big slice of the credit. I know your career as a sports writer will go from strength to strength.

Stuart's uncle, Barry Lewis, volunteered to proofread all of the chapters. This was a wonderful gesture, but one he tackled with professionalism and pride—he, too, is a Newcastle United supporter, like many fans featured on our pages. Thank you, Barry. You and your family have been a wonderful support to this project.

Angie and friends with Supermac poster, Wembley 1976

Thanks to all of my family and friends who have kept the faith, and encouraged me. Special thanks to the fabulous Ruth Askey (The Passion P.A.) who has worked tirelessly transcribing interviews, and acting as a wonderful host for some of the many and varied guests at our table who loved her company–despite, shall we say, her football knowledge not being quite as wide-ranging as it might be!

Thanks also to my good friend Susan Purves, who has joined me both home and away over the years. We have some great football memories and hopefully many more to come. Thanks Susan, you have encouraged me every step of the way.

HALL OF FANS

northern rock

13

wonga
SPORTSDIRECT

SL BENFICA
4 DE ABRIL ESTÁDIO DA LUZ
NEWCASTLE UTD
11 DE ABRIL ST. JAMES' PARK

MIKE
ON
TOUR

COCA-COLA CHAMPIONSHIP
CHAMPIONS 2009/10

NEWCASTLE UNITED

OLYMPIQUE
LYONNAIS
JUVENTUS
TOON ARMY

FIRE EXIT

A Poetry Notebook

MAGS

United

9

money

northern
rock

NEWCASTLE UNITED

northern rock

UNITED
Bukta

17
United

18

N U
C

wonga

18

CELEBRITY FOOTBALL
PASSION
®